Treasures of Alaska

LAST GREAT AMERICAN WILDERNESS

All feathers and fury, a bald eagle swoops through the Alaskan sky.
Previous page: A Tlingit artist carved "The Lookout," a living trail marker atop Mount Roberts.

Scanning the waters off Point Adolphus, whale-watchers look for signs of humpbacks.

Ice from South Sawyer Glacier drifts in the emerald waters of Tracy Arm.

Flashes of sunlight add fleeting brush strokes of color to the sky over Punchbowl Lake

Treasures
of Alaska

LAST GREAT AMERICAN WILDERNESS

JEFF RENNICKE

PHOTOGRAPHS BY
MICHAEL MELFORD

NATIONAL
GEOGRAPHIC

WASHINGTON, D.C.

Chukchi
Sea

Siberia

RUSSIA

Chukchi
Peninsula

Noatak

CAPE
KRUSENSTERN
N.M.

ARCTIC CIRCLE

Kotzebue

Bering
Strait

Shishmaref

BERING
LAND
BRIDGE
N.P.

Serpentine
Hot Springs

Seward
Peninsula

Nome

Gambell

Savoonga

St. Lawrence
Island

0   miles   200
0   kilometers   300

YUKON

DELTA   *Yukon*

NATIONAL

WILDLIFE

Bethel

REFUGE

TOGIAK
NATIONAL
WILDLIFE
REFUGE

WALRUS IS.
STATE GAME
SANCTUARY

Bristol
Bay

Bering

Sea

St. Paul

Pribilof
Islands

A
l
e
u
t
i
a
n

Buldir I.

Islands

Pavlof Volcano
8,261 ft

Unimak
Island

Shishaldin Volcano
9,372 ft

Makushin Volcano
6,680 ft

Akutan Peak
4,275 ft

Mt. Okmok
3,519 ft

Unalaska

Unalaska I.

Tulik Volcano
4,111 ft

Umnak I.

PACIFIC   OCEAN

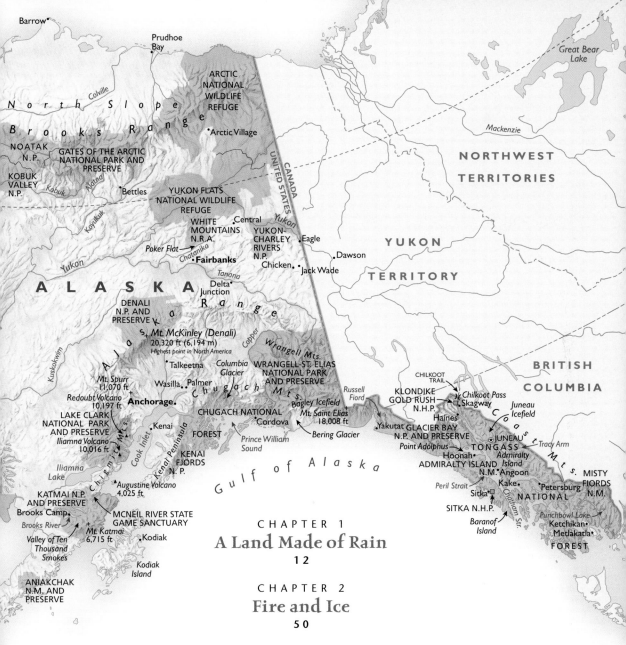

CHAPTER 1

A Land Made of Rain

Rain is falling. But this is not a passing thunderstorm, with its dramatic rolling and rumbling. Water falls from the sky slowly, gently, and ceaselessly, as if it could go on for days, or years. Rain soaks deep into the forest floor, making the moss squish beneath hiking boots. It drips, drips, drips off the tips of leaves, nodding the blossoms of wildflowers with the weight of each drop. Waterfalls are singing. And still there is rain: 150 inches a year in Ketchikan on Revillagigedo Island, 224 inches at Little Port Walter on the south shore of Baranof Island, even more in the mountains above.

The world, it seems, has turned to water.

On the M.V. *Aurora*, windshield wipers streak a moment of that rain off the pilothouse windows as Captain George Brereton steers the 235-foot ferry north at 14 knots through the calm waters of Clarence Strait near Ketchikan. With 67 passengers aboard and 21 vehicles on her car deck, the *Aurora* is making an early season run. We will visit six more ports after Ketchikan—Petersburg, Kake, Sitka, Angoon, Hoonah, and Juneau—in 39 hours, longer if we are lucky. "I've stopped ships for deer swimming the channel, for bears along the shore, and to give whales the right-of-way," says Captain Brereton. "You never know what we might see."

Of the 14 communities served by the marine highway system of Southeast Alaska, only the mainland towns of Haines and Skagway are connected to the outside world by roads. The rest rely on the "Blue Canoe" to bring fresh fish, groceries, and other supplies and to transport friends and family members. In this part of the state, even Santa Claus comes to town every Christmas riding on a ferry.

The *Aurora* is a spartan vessel without staterooms or berths, so passengers set up tents on the open decks or wrap themselves in blankets on plastic deck chairs in the solarium. On this trip two elderly sisters from Angoon are returning from a baby shower "outside," which to an Alaskan means anywhere outside of the state. Also on board is a fisherman heading for Sitka with his three-year-old son, who wears miniature versions of his dad's red suspenders and knee-high rubber boots.

Most of the passengers this time of year—late spring—are visitors or seasonal workers going north, some of them for the first time. Patrick, on his first trip to Alaska, is heading for a summer job in Denali National Park and Preserve. A retired couple from Florida have volunteered as campground hosts in a state park near Anchorage. Sean, a college kid as fresh-faced as a crisp dollar bill, carries a backpack and a recently bought guidebook; he sports a scratchy new haircut and hiking boots right out of the box. "Going to Alaska," he says several times as if he can't quite believe it himself. "Going to Alaska."

Ahead, through the rain-streaked windows of the observation deck, lie the 450 sea-blue, spruce-green miles of Southeast Alaska, the long, narrow panhandle that trails south and east from the main body of the state. This is where Alaska begins for the hundreds of thousands of visitors who travel up the Inside Passage each year by cruise ship or ferry. It begins with the dot-dash of a thousand islands, the white-capped mountains rising in waves against the mainland, and the slow *shushing* of surf in countless coves. It begins in the white ribbons of fog gift-wrapping the deep bays of Misty Fiords National Monument and in the hundred-year-old silence of a stand of old-growth trees in Tongass National Forest. It begins with totem poles, fishing boats, and bald eagles decorating the branches of a spruce like brown-and-white Christmas ornaments.

On the *Aurora*, loudspeakers suddenly crackle to life with the voice of chief purser Jim Beedle: "Humpback whales have been spotted off the starboard side." We line up elbow-to-elbow along the rail, watching as a beam of sunlight breaks through the clouds and turns the water to a glimmer of silver, broken only by the outlines of three whales working their way up the channel.

Each spring Alaska fills with life again. In the far north, caribou begin to move, the dark strings of the herds pulling the season up the mountains behind them. All across the state, bears wake from their long winter's sleep to stitch the late snows with their tracks. Over the Alaskan interior, skies fill with wings as millions of pintail, snow geese, dunlins, sandpipers, swans, cranes, and songbirds move north with the light to nest. Along the coast, salmon swirl in the river mouths.

And here in Southeast Alaska whales are swimming again in the bays. The three humpbacks slide through the water, keeping pace with the ferry, which has slowed to give us a better look. About 40 feet long and weighing 40 tons, they move as gracefully as curved light in the water, their slick, black backs rising and falling like dark wing beats until finally they show their tails and dive. Alaska begins here, too, in the flick of a whale's tail sending a spray of water high into the air, a spray that falls like raindrops back into the sea.

Near Sitka, rain still falls as I walk through a forest of eyes belonging to whales, ravens, bears, beavers, and wolves. I see a sea monster known as Waasgo and a village watchman wrapped by fog in a shawl of gray. All are carved in wood in the totem poles at Sitka National Historical Park.

Such carvings have been made for centuries by the Tlingit, Haida, and Tsimshian peoples. With no written language, families and clans created totem poles to record their stories. Poles were carved to honor the dead and to display clan crests. They were a way to announce what clan was living in the area and to commemorate important events such as marriages or births, battles or floods. They were even a means for a clan to ridicule enemies. The poles were, in essence, a carved history.

"Totem poles were never worshiped," says Nathan Jackson, a master carver who lives near Saxman in the greater Ketchikan area. "That's one of the biggest misconceptions. They are more like images of George Washington or Abraham Lincoln. You don't bow down to these men or to their images, which help tell stories about each man's character or the country's history. It is the same with the figures on totem poles."

Carvings show Raven being swallowed by a whale, a strongman named Stone Ribs escaping the underworld in the belly of a seal, Creek Woman returning the salmon to the streams each spring, and more. These stories, like the poles themselves, seem to spring straight from the natural world, born of forests and rain and time. Before the introduction of iron and steel tools, people used blades of jadeite, knives of copper and sharpened clamshell, and chisels of beaver teeth to carve poles. Painted with colors made from minerals such as ocher, manganese, and graphite, totem poles were raised during potlatches, elaborate ceremonies that usually lasted for days.

With the introduction of steel tools, totem pole carving reached an apex in the 1860s and '70s. By the end of the century, as many as 600 poles were thought to stand in Southeast Alaska. Some villages fairly bristled with them; in 1916 the abandoned village of Tuxekan alone counted as many as 125. But as missionaries moved in, native peoples were urged to turn their backs on traditional ways and beliefs. Totem poles, the most visible and dramatic symbol of those ways, were chopped down, sold, cut up for firewood, even dynamited by newcomers. Over the years, the few poles that remained began to topple and crumble in the rain. An art form was vanishing in the mist.

"The damp weather of Southeast Alaska can be tough on totem poles," said Claudia Vargas when I visited Ketchikan's Totem Heritage Center earlier in the trip. Striving to perpetuate and strengthen the cultures of native peoples, this center is a valuable resource for carvers who wish to study old totem poles. As Vargas led me through its climate-controlled storage rooms, I saw, resting on shelf after shelf, more than a dozen badly deteriorated poles as fragile as moth wings, some so rotted they were pieced together like jigsaw puzzles.

Ferries and fishing boats alike travel the Inside Passage, Southeast Alaska's "liquid main street." The region has thousands of miles of coastline and almost no roads.

Following pages: Named for the mist that cloaks its bays, Misty Fiords National Monument protects a fraction of Alaska's more than 326 million acres of public land, much of it accessible only by boat, foot, or bush plane.

"The life span of an untreated pole left out in the elements is about 70 years," Vargas told me as I stared into a barely discernible eye carved by unknown hands over a century ago. "The poles in our collection are 100 to 160 years old. If they hadn't been brought in, they would be long gone by now."

And that's not just because of damp weather. "Look at this one," she said, pointing to the Fog Woman pole encased in glass. "When surveyors first cataloged it at Village Island, they saw bullet holes where someone had used it for target practice. When they came back again, they found that vandals had tried to cut off the main crest with a saw."

The territorial government collected several dozen poles in the 1890s and 1900s for display at what is now Sitka National Historical Park. In 1938 the Civilian Conservation Corps hired young men to make replicas of totem poles under the tutelage of master carvers. That project, a major reason for the art's survival, involved the creation of reproductions at Mud Bight, which later became Totem Bight State Park. The Totem Heritage Center, built in 1976, houses 33 original poles; it is Alaska's largest collection of unaltered poles recovered in the 1970s from Tlingit sites in Tongass and on Village Island, and from the Haida community of Old (Continued on page 26)

"The hazards of flying bush are numerous," says pilot Michelle Masden during takeoff from Misty Fiords National Monument (above). "You must deal with rain, fog, wind, and tides." But the reward, she says, "is flying in the most beautiful place on Earth."

Opposite: To touch the Tongass National Forest, you have to get your feet wet and taste the rain like these passengers aboard the M.V. *Liseron,* enjoying a mist-in-the-face view of a waterfall in Tracy Arm.

Ravaged by time and weather, a totem pole such as this one near Saxman can sink into the wet forest floor in less than a lifetime. As poles fade away, so do stories their creators carved upon them. "Many of the stories totem poles once told, we will simply never know," says Claudia Vargas of the Totem Heritage Center.

Stories still live on intact totem poles, including one about a raven (above). Retrieved from villages and copied by the Civilian Conservation Corps in the 1930s, more than a dozen such poles remain on display at Saxman, south of Ketchikan.

Following pages: "Totem poles put us on the map. They speak of who we are," says Nathan Jackson, a Tlingit master carver at work in the carving shed at Saxman.

(Continued from page 17) Kasaan. Collecting the poles was controversial; in native traditions, they were never moved or repaired once they were in place. At Totem Heritage Center a plaque quotes Dennis Demmert of the Alaska Native Brotherhood, a sponsor of the 1969 recovery effort: "Preservation was a new idea to us…but we decided that in the interest of preserving the bit of our heritage that remained, we would try to save the poles."

In doing so, they may also have saved an art form. "A lot of carvers were needed to repair the old poles and produce replicas," says Nathan Jackson, who worked on many of the poles now displayed at Totem Bight and has carved new poles for the Totem Heritage Center. "There wasn't anyone left who remembered the old techniques, so things needed to be relearned, old tools reinvented." The recovery effort spawned a new generation of carvers who took up where others had left off. One of them was Jackson.

"I started out wanting to be a fisherman," says Jackson, born into the Sockeye Clan of the Chilkoot Tlingit. But a 55-day hospital stay after breathing in paint dust and jellyfish powder while disk-sanding a boat hull changed his plans. "To pass the time, I carved little totem poles in the scraps of yellow cedar left over in the occupational therapy room. I filled a whole showcase with them," he says. By the time he got out of the hospital, the fishing season was over but his carving career had just begun.

Today, with more than 30 totem poles to his credit, Nathan Jackson is an internationally renowned carver. His artwork is included in every major Alaskan museum. It is on display throughout the United States and in collections as far-flung as Europe, Australia, and Japan. He has won a National Endowment for the Arts fellowship and has been awarded an honorary doctorate of humanities from the University of Alaska. He is considered a "living cultural treasure" for his artistry in wood. Still, he only smiles when I call him an artist. "The Tlingit language has no word for art," he says. "Sometimes I feel more like a trailblazer, going back to brush out a trail that almost disappeared so that it could be followed again." To ensure that the trail stretches into the future, Jackson teaches classes in carving and takes on apprentices in the craft. He bristles at having once been called "the last" Tlingit carver. "I had a pretty negative reaction to that," he says. "With all the people I've taken under my wing, there is a long line of carvers on the horizon."

One of them is Jackson's son Stephen, whose first major totem pole was recently unveiled in the Mount Roberts Tramway building on the Juneau waterfront. "The biggest challenge for carvers today," Stephen says while putting the final touches on a pole honoring the Auk Clan of Juneau, "is to find the right balance between respecting the symbols of the past and developing your own style. As with any art form, to stay vibrant and alive, totem pole carving has to continue to evolve. It has to be as much about our lives in the present and the future as it is about the past."

No one can know just how much of that past was lost. In all of Southeast Alaska, only a few totem poles are still standing on the sites where they were originally raised. Yet the Tsimshian have raised several new poles in recent years at the village of Metlakatla on Annette Island. A 35-foot pole carved in 1996 at the Sitka National Historical Park now stands as the first traditional pole raised by the Sitka Tlingit in more than a hundred years.

As a new generation of carvers takes up the work and local peoples experience a renewed sense of cultural pride, it is not hard at all to imagine on a foggy morning walk that the trail through the forest of eyes leads as much toward the future as it does to the past.

The rain has stopped, for now, but ahead of us lies water of another kind: ice. Even in June the green water of Tracy Arm sparkles with ice. The path, clogged with icebergs, "looks like a minefield," someone says. "Aye, laddie," replies Captain Steve Tarrant of the M.V. *Observer* in his best fake accent. "But we be in a minesweeper!"

After leaving the ferry at Juneau, I have booked passage on the *Observer*, a wooden-hulled, World War II-era minesweeper converted into a 12-passenger cruising vessel. A smaller and more maneuverable ship, with a shallow draft, the 100-foot *Observer* can explore areas that ferries and cruise ships rarely reach. "Six days," says first mate Larry Funner, "and we don't stop at a single T-shirt shop!" Instead, we explore the coastal reaches of the Tongass National Forest.

Blurring the line between myth and reality, a raven carved atop a totem pole at Saxman appears to come to life and soar. Trickster, elder, and bringer of fire, the raven takes many forms in age-old stories.

More than 75 percent of Southeast Alaska lies within the Tongass National Forest. At 16.9 million acres, the Tongass could hide West Virginia among its peaks and riverbeds, yet the forest has very few long hiking trails and almost no public road system. It does have more than a thousand islands, 11,000 miles of coastline, and 45,000 miles of streams. Admiralty Island, known as Kootznoowoo or "fortress of the bear" to the Tlingit, is home to North America's highest documented concentration of brown bears, like the mother and two cubs we see along the shore, dark as shadows, plucking lip-red thimbleberries one by one. From just a few yards offshore, we can see the juice of the berries running red on the dark fur of their faces.

The Tongass has glaciers, too. Sawyer and South Sawyer Glaciers lie like strands of bluish white pearls at the end of Tracy Arm, a 25-mile-long inlet with a lightning bolt shape. Dark granite walls rise several thousand feet on either side, their cliffs strung with the long, white strings of waterfalls. Mountain goats drift white against the rocky slopes.

The *Observer* weaves among the icebergs to within half a mile of the jagged blue face of South Sawyer Glacier. It then unloads a small skiff piloted by Colleen Dunseth, the ship's naturalist, who will take us even closer. Dunseth gave up a job as the captain of her own fishing boat because, she says, "I wanted to help people appreciate all the wildness, all the beauty that I was seeing every day from my fishing boat." She is smiling, for this is exactly what she had in mind.

Soon we are surrounded by ice, a kaleidoscope of icebergs that change shape with every angle—a pillar, a human face, a bird frozen in flight. The air is as cool as peppermint against our teeth. Shafts of sunlight poking through the clouds throw spotlights, making each iceberg in turn seem to glow with the blue of a summer sky or the silver-gray of smoked glass.

Staring at the infinity of ice, I think of David Rosenthal. This well-known Alaskan landscape painter from Cordova captures glaciers on canvas. "I spent years looking for a tube of paint that color blue," he told me once. "But it doesn't exist." Neither do the shapes and figures of the ice he paints, or at least people don't think they do. "I just paint what I see," he shrugged. "But no matter how realistically I depict the ice, people who've never seen a glacier think it can't possibly be like that, and they take it as abstract art anyway."

Many of the ice floes are peppered with harbor seals, which raise their heads to follow our progress as we use oars to push aside smaller bergs to clear a path. "The seals come up to the heads of fjords like this to give birth on the ice away from the orcas," says Dunseth. "Over a hundred do so here in Tracy Arm," she says. "Orcas, or killer whales, are the wolf packs of the sea. They hunt in groups, sometimes taking on prey as large as minke or gray whales. They've been seen working in tandem to tip resting seals off ice floes. One will shove the side of the iceberg up until the seal rolls off the other side, right into the mouth of the other orca. When seals see them coming, they'll do anything to get out of the water."

Anything. In Glacier Bay National Park and Preserve, where a thousand harbor seals give birth in Johns Hopkins Inlet, naturalist Dena Matkin once sat watching as a group of killer whales circled a seal, driving it near her boat off Willoughby Island. Without any ice floes nearby, the seal kept coming closer and closer to the only thing floating on the water—Matkin's boat. "She came close enough for me to reach out my hand and stroke her head," Matkin told me. At that point, the seal decided that even a human was infinitely better company than killer whales and climbed right up into the boat. "She just lay there on the bottom of the boat for a while and then, when the whales gave up, jumped back into the water and swam away."

With no orcas in sight in Tracy Arm, a glistening seal bobs and weaves to within a few feet of our skiff. The creature periscopes its head up, eyes as dark as deep pools of water; then—plop—it quickly is gone, leaving behind a small ring of ripples that clatter in the ice crystals like wind through chimes.

The wind is moaning in the treetops and swaying the branches as the *Observer*, with us safely back on board, turns west out of Chatham Strait into the long, deep, protected arms of Warm Springs Bay. For centuries people have been tucking into this bay on the east side of Baranof Island to fish at the 40-foot falls at its head, to soak in its hot springs, and to wait out storms.

The rickety wooden dock is already filling with colorful, wave-battered fishing boats. We drop anchor in the bay and wait while the radio crackles with news of an approaching storm—who is tucking into what bay, making the run for port ahead of the storm, or planning to try to ride it out.

Cold and remote, Alaskan waters are some of the most difficult in the world to fish, but they are also some of the richest: In a single good season, fishermen take from the sea more wealth than was found in the Klondike gold rush a century ago. Each year the commercial fishing industry nets the largest catch of any fishery in the United States, both in value and in sheer volume. That catch—about five billion pounds of fish and shellfish, including salmon, crab, halibut, and cod—is half of all the seafood landed in the U.S. and worth more than a billion dollars. In terms of economic value, commercial fishing is the third largest industry in the state, after oil and tourism. It is first in terms of employment, responsible for 47 percent of all private-sector jobs.

But fishing does not come without a price. "It is the most dangerous job in Alaska," attorney and part-time fish-buyer Bruce Weyhrauch tells me. With the harsh seas, unpredictable weather, and immense distances between safe harbors, an average of 24 lives and 34 boats are lost each year. "And that fact gets very little recognition," he says. "When a good friend died in a fishing accident in 1989, I found out there wasn't a memorial anywhere in the state to honor all the people who have been lost through the years."

Weyhrauch and others set out to establish the Alaska Commercial Fishermen's Memorial that stands today on the Juneau waterfront. The curved wall of granite is carved with the names of 119 fishermen who lost their lives in the waters of Southeast Alaska. The memorial is also the site of the annual blessing of the fleet, which is held each May. *(Continued on page 40)*

Following pages: Ice from the Columbia Glacier thrills kayakers but can threaten ships in Prince William Sound.

Pages 32-33: Frozen in time? In chilly waters at the foot of the Columbia Glacier, a kayaker gets his picture taken inside an iceberg.

Rich in more than scenery, Alaska accounts for 94 percent of the Pacific salmon harvested in the United States, an abundance that provides a livelihood for 12,000 commercial fishermen—including, perhaps, people on this boat near Point Adolphus. "It's rare that you see a fisherman retire," says Barbara Cadiente-Nelson, whose family runs fishing boats out of Juneau's docks. "Fishing's too much a part of who people are."

More than 3,000 rivers, including this one on the Kenai Peninsula, flow through the landscapes of Alaska. They hold five species of Pacific salmon and provide a respite for sport fishermen, who in 1999 took 1.4 million salmon and caught and released 1.7 million more.

Following pages: With a wave of its tail, a humpback dives deep in Chatham Strait. Once almost lost to commercial whaling, humpbacks continue making a slow recovery; about 4,000 spend the summer in Alaska's waters.

Long-liners—fishing vessels that string 2,000 feet of line in one pass across the ocean floor—annually haul in nearly 50 million pounds of halibut, one of the state's most important commercial fish species.

Opposite: In Misty Fiords National Monument, a rickety old boardwalk along Punchbowl Lake leads visitors into the largest and most intact temperate rain forest left on the planet.

(Continued from page 29)   Prayers are offered and names of the departed are solemnly read as family members place flowers against the stone. A wreath is set afloat and, one by one, fishing boats pass by for a ceremonial sprinkling of holy water, boats such as the *Aleut Princess* run by Barbara Cadiente-Nelson.

"The blessing of the fleet recognizes a large part of who we are in terms of our contribution to the state's economy," says Cadiente-Nelson, who with her sons, husband, and father-in-law runs fishing vessels out of Juneau. They work the waters of the Southeast, the Gulf of Alaska, and Bristol Bay. "Perhaps even more important, the event brings awareness of the fact that the food some people take for granted is brought to market at a great expense not just in terms of money spent but in human lives as well," she adds.

"It's not easy work. Increased regulations give us less and less time to fish, often leaving us only horrific weather to fish in, and then prices are so low for what you do bring in," she tells me. "No matter how much gear you run or how long you stay at it, you just seem to be pulling your foot out of one mud hole and putting it in another."

Fishing will be more difficult for Barbara Cadiente-Nelson and her family this year. On August 24, 2000, the *Aleut Princess* burned to the waterline and sank in Chatham Strait off Admiralty Island's Danger Point. "That boat was a tough old taskmaster, getting us through more storms than I can count," she says. Though no one was hurt, the vessel was a total loss. Still they will go on. "Most people who fish don't care to do anything else," says Cadiente-Nelson, whose sons represent the fourth generation of fishermen on their father's side and the next generation in a long line on her side, which includes Aleut and Tlingit forebears. "I never intended for my children to make their living this way, but now I realize that fishing is too much a part of who they are for them to stop. We'll endure to the bitter end, even with the loss of the *Aleut Princess*."

Inexplicably, the storm misses us, slides to the south. By morning the fishing boats have all headed out, and the *Observer* is the last to leave the bay. "*Alaska Song, Alaska Song....* This is the *Observer*, over." Captain Tarrant hails a friend to check conditions in Sitkoh Bay as we steam north again under glacier-blue skies. "Oh, we're just miserable out here," *Alaska Song* mocks. "We can't keep the salmon out of the boat. Rough seas all of about two or three inches. The sun is shining. Yeah, pretty darn miserable."

We take advantage of that "miserable" weather to anchor in a shallow bay off Peril Strait and go for a hike. Only a few steps from shore we are swallowed by forest, our every footfall muffled by moss. Shafts of sunlight flicker through the branches like light through stained glass windows.

"This is the real Tongass," Steve Tarrant says as we step into a grove of ancient trees strung with long strands of lichen known as old man's beard.

The Tongass National Forest includes part of the largest temperate rain forest left on Earth; it is an ecological treasure, its hidden groves humming with life. Here, Sitka black-tailed deer move ghostlike on their tiny hooves, marbled murrelets lay eggs on beds of moss in old-growth trees, and flowers use the splash of raindrops to disperse their pollen.

Four of us stretch our arms out wide and link hands, just barely encircling the trunk of an immense Sitka spruce, a tree that Richard Carstensen and Sam Skaggs would love. In 1996 Skaggs, a sailboat captain, and Carstensen, a well-respected naturalist, began the Landmark Tree Project to search out and map the largest, most ancient trees in stands of old-growth forest within the Tongass. So far, the oldest tree they have found is a yellow cedar, while the largest is a Sitka spruce.

"You walk into some of these forests and it is literally like walking into a cathedral," Skaggs says in a reverent tone. "You speak more quietly. You move more slowly, with the unmistakable feeling of being somewhere very ancient. Some of the trees have huge bear scratches, and there are broken-off snags as thick as your waist. Eagle nests look like they've been there for decades. It is a very powerful experience to be among the big trees."

Rising about 180 feet, a 400-year-old Sitka spruce measures 9, 10, or even 11 feet in diameter at chest height. Younger but taller trees have also been found: One of the landmark plots holds four 240-foot giants, each topped by a crown having a 25-foot radius. The oldest trees tend to be shorter than others of their species because over the years wind has blown out their tops.

According to Skaggs, his quest involves more than just a hunt for the biggest trees. "There is a certain Guinness element to it, I know," he says. "But what we are really hoping to do is use the big trees as a way to talk about the full ecology of the rain forest: how rich it is and what an important niche these old-growth stands fill. The salmon, brown bears, Sitka black-tailed deer, old-growth forest—they're all interrelated. You can't have one without the other. Nature doesn't work that way. I don't think people realize how important these last stands of old-growth forest are to the ecological integrity of the Tongass."

They will if Skaggs has his way. "I'd like to elevate these trees in the eyes of the visitor to the same level of excitement as the 'big three' that tourists always want to see. I'd like people to go home after their trip and say they saw a bear, a glacier, a whale, and, oh yeah, one of those landmark trees, too."

Sitting in the stillness of an ancient grove, one is tempted to think of the rain forest as unbroken and unbreakable wilderness. It is not. Although 5.8 million acres of the Tongass now make up 19 designated wilderness areas, decades of intense logging on other sections—spurred by unprecedented long-term timber contracts and federally subsidized timber sales—have "just about cut the heart out of the forest," according to Buck Lindekugel of the Southeast Alaska Conservation Council.

Over a million acres of state, private, and federal lands have been clear-cut in Southeast Alaska. Nearly half of the prime old-growth timber stands in the Tongass have already gone under the chain saw in the last 50 years; many of them have been lost to clear-cutting, a logging method that Lindekugel says threatens salmon streams and wildlife habitat, adds silt to the streams, and erodes the other values of forestland. "The Forest Service has this multiple-use mantra," Lindekugel says. "But the clear-cuts aren't multiple use. You're not going to go hunt in a clear-cut or go fish or picnic. People won't hike or camp there."

That's what also worries Captain Steve Tarrant. "We are not completely against logging," he tells me when we are back on board the *Observer* and cruising through Peril Strait. From the pilot-house we can see old clear-cuts scarring the hillsides. "But we do oppose large-scale clear-cuts that don't take into account the ecological health of the forest or the needs of those who make their living through tourism. People come to Southeast Alaska to see the natural beauty and wildlife," he says. "Who is going to come all the way up here just to see the clear-cuts?"

In the forests near Ketchikan, tiny grottoes and small falls such as this one (opposite) near the Deer Mountain National Recreation Trail support a rich mosaic of life.

Following pages: Fireweed spreads like wildfire across a field in Mendenhall Valley, north of Juneau.

During our last morning as passengers on the *Observer*, my 12-year-old daughter Katelyn and I go ashore for some exploring. Strolling along, I watch her walk unaware toward a stream that is roiling with spawning salmon. She steps too quickly to the edge, and the stream suddenly erupts with fish, their tails whipping the water white with foam. Katelyn prances back toward me, laughing and splashing water up over her boots.

"A lot of people come to Southeast Alaska and never get past the gift shops on the cruise ships," Steve Tarrant had said to me earlier. "But when you get off the ship and touch this place, roll up your sleeves and stick your arm elbow deep in a mossy log, or see a grizzly track in the mud, you become engaged with this place. You have to feel the rain. You have to get your feet wet. Then it's like plugging into the 220. That's the raw feed."

I can see a bit of that "raw feed" buzzing in my daughter's eyes as we walk back toward the *Observer*, which is floating quietly in a shallow bay off Peril Strait. The clouds have come down, and a soft rain has begun to fall from them. While some raindrops plink like musical notes off the countless shells lying at the edge of the tide line, others splatter quietly on the calm water in the bay. Raindrops also slosh about in our rubber boots, though we hardly seem to notice.

The rain is falling again in a land made of rain. ▲

Surrounding more than a thousand islands and filling countless streams, water takes many forms in southeastern and south-central Alaska. It gently touches the shores of Prince William Sound at sunset (opposite) and chatters raucously in Bridal Veil Falls (above).

Following pages: To dry their feathers, cormorants stand atop rocks and bask in the day's last rays of light.

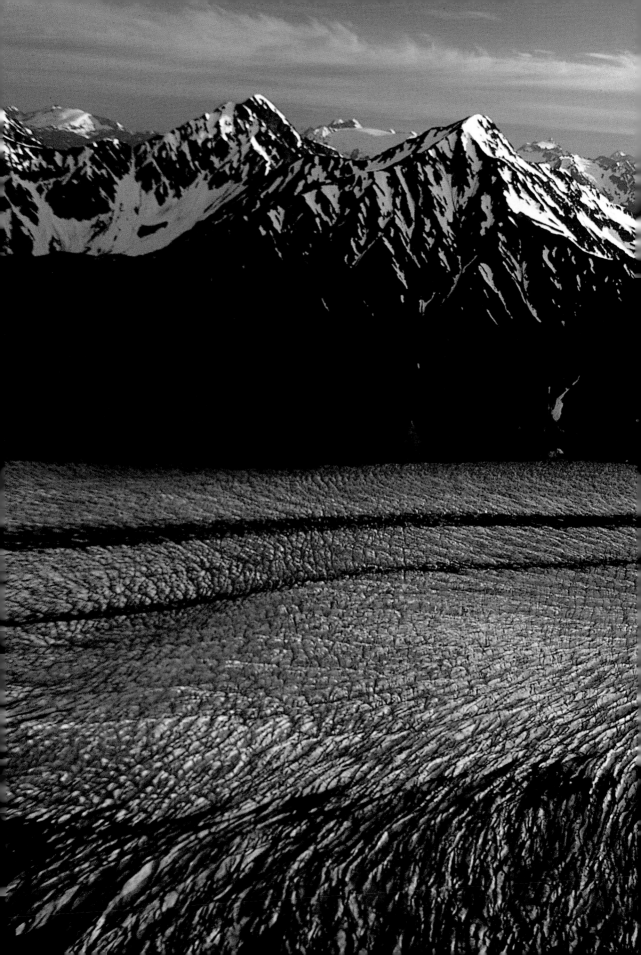

CHAPTER 2

Fire and Ice

A gust of cold wind gathers in the growing darkness and hurtles out across the ice. Four thousand feet up in the Coast Mountains, I pull the collar snug on my jacket and ski faster, trying to stay warm. It is the 27th of July, high summer far below, yet snowflakes still swirl in thick curtains, and peaks thick with drifts poke like dark fangs through the ice all around me. Winter remains locked tight on these mountains northeast of Juneau as six of us ski down the Southwest Branch and out onto the broad back of the Taku Glacier. This is the Juneau Icefield, where glaciers are born.

According to estimates, more than 100,000 glaciers glitter across Alaska, nestling high in the cirques of the Brooks Range or cascading through the cold, stone valleys of the Chugach Mountains to calve into the sea. Some are tiny and nameless, visited only by the wind. Others are immense: The Bering Glacier–Bagley Icefield covers 2,250 square miles, nearly twice the area of Rhode Island. Each summer, tidewater glaciers in Prince William Sound and along the Inside Passage thrill cruise-ship passengers with the white fireworks of their calving. Portage Glacier, southeast of Anchorage, and Mendenhall Glacier, near Juneau, are two of the most popular attractions in the state.

These great rivers of ice can fashion spectacular landscapes. In Glacier Bay National Park and Preserve, ice has retreated 65 miles from where it was 200 years ago, creating the "solitude of ice and snow and newborn rocks" once admired by naturalist John Muir. Land in the Bartlett Cove region, site of park headquarters, is so recently unburdened from the weight of ice that it is rebounding an inch and a half a year, rising as if taking a long, slow breath.

Alaska's glaciers appear in legends as well as landscapes: A tale from Hoonah says that the beckoning of a lonely little girl caused glaciers to advance down what the Tlingit people called Tcukanedi, or "valley of the river of grass." Villagers living in the path of the ice were forced to flee to the coast.

Glaciers also teach us about the Earth's history, about our climate, and ultimately about ourselves.

"Can anyone tell me what we can learn from the rock we are standing on?" asks Maynard Miller, one of the world's leading experts on glaciers. He has gathered a group of students on a granite outcrop that juts above the Taku Glacier like a stage. About a thousand feet below is the scattering of buildings known as Camp 10, one of a string of camps used each summer by the Juneau Icefield Research Program (JIRP) founded by Miller.

At 79, he has spent a lifetime in the mountains. He led the first American ascent of Mount St. Elias in 1946 and served as chief geologist on the 1963 American Everest Expedition; for more than 50 years Maynard Miller has returned each summer to teach and do research on the Juneau Icefield. In his eyes, the landscape is an open book: Stories are written everywhere, including on the rock where we are standing.

"Remember," he says, repeating one of his favorite slogans, "don't just look. See!" Gray-haired, eyes flashing, ice ax in hand, and perched on a rock stage high in the mountains, he looks almost biblical, all but trembling with his desire for students to understand.

"Do you mean…the lines?" someone ventures tentatively, pointing to a set of scratch marks on the rock.

"Yes!" Miller nearly explodes. "Glacial striae!" From just a few scratches, he paints a picture of how this rock was overrun twice by glacial ice, which came from different directions, at different times and depths. Once the ice buried the mountain behind us; another time it flowed around, forming a nunatak, or rock island surrounded by ice. "It's all here," he says. "Nature is screaming at us. You just have to learn to understand what it's showing you."

Founded in 1946, JIRP is the longest-running ice-field research program in the world. Students are challenged scientifically, academically, and physically. "It's the Emersonian triangle—books, nature, action," Miller says. "Our fundamental aim is leadership training, to strengthen the cadre of field scientists in the United States." Each summer 70 to 100 students, researchers, staff, and faculty come from all over the world to attend camp lectures, rappel into crevasses, ski over untracked ice, and climb windblown slopes to poke, prod, and learn the secrets of the ice. They also learn about themselves.

Previous pages: Fueled by prodigious winter snows, 24 named glaciers, including the Bear Glacier shown here, cascade off the 300-square-mile Harding Icefield that caps Kenai Fjords National Park.

"Experiences near or beyond the boundary of your skill level make you better," says Miller, nodding toward a group of students using crampons and ice axes to work their way down a steep slope. "These students learn the skills and then test those boundaries throughout the summer, growing not only as field research scientists but also as human beings." Their classroom is 5,000 square miles of ice and rock.

On a day with a sky as white as the ice, I join researcher Scott McGee and graduate student Susan Kaspari as they set a line of survey stakes across the Taku Glacier; the stakes will be resurveyed in five days to determine the glacier's rate of movement. All day McGee and I have been riding in a Thiokol, an orange over-the-snow vehicle, while Kaspari—operating a global positioning system (GPS)—has stood behind us on a sled protected from the elements by a makeshift plastic shelter and which we affectionately call the "popemobile." But our ride has just come to an end.

"Uh, oh. I don't like the look of this," McGee says. Ahead, the ice is scrimshawed with the blue lines of pressure cracks and deep crevasses. "We'll have to rope up and ski."

With a long climbing rope clipped between us, we ski gingerly out into the jumbled ice. All around us is the sound of running water. "One of the Thiokols fell into a crevasse a few years back. Did I tell you that?" Scott smiles as we weave our way among meltwater ponds and jagged crevasses filled with bottomless blue-black light. "No one was hurt, but it took a couple of weeks to take the thing apart piece by piece and hoist it back onto the surface."

To keep my mind off crevasses, I ask Scott about the movement of the Taku Glacier. "The flow rate of the Taku has been remarkably consistent over the years," he says. "Each day it moves about a meter, something like 93 centimeters, at this location." By comparison, some Alaskan glaciers fairly gallop down their valleys: In 1936 and 1937, Black Rapids Glacier south of Delta Junction became known as "the galloping glacier" when it surged three miles in six months, threatening Richardson Highway. In 1956 and 1957, Muldrow Glacier on the northeast side of Mount McKinley advanced as much as 1,150 feet a day. More recently, Bering Glacier in the Chugach Mountains gave researchers an unprecedented scientific opportunity—and a little excitement.

Bruce Molnia of the U.S. Geological Survey has studied the Bering Glacier for more than a decade, and in July 1994 he had a crew out along Tsiu Lake's southwest shore, at the glacier's edge. "About midday," he says, "they felt the ground start to shake. At first they thought it was an earthquake, but the ground kept shaking." Climbing a ridge to get a better view, they saw huge chunks of ice being tossed into the air. Something was ripping apart North America's largest and longest glacier, and it was doing so right before their eyes.

"By the time we got there," Molnia recalls, "we saw that the entire face of the glacier was being torn apart by a huge jet of water shooting 200 meters straight out from the base, right at waterline." A sediment dam that had blocked the outflow—pooling water in, on, and under the ice—had given way and set off a glacial outburst flood of epic proportions. "It was louder than Niagara Falls. House- and bus-size blocks of ice were being knocked off. Icebergs, some of them 15 meters high, would drift in front of the jet and literally disappear." In just 24 hours the force of the water carved a chasm in the ice hundreds of feet deep and a quarter mile long.

The event was but one part of a three-year burst of activity in which the glacier surged up to 300 feet a day, advancing six miles in places, and Molnia and his team were there to document it. "This was the first time a surge cycle of this magnitude has been watched from its inception through its conclusion, and now we are watching the aftermath," he says. "It taught us, and continues to teach us, a tremendous amount about the ever changing dynamics of glaciers. We didn't have to just sit and wonder how this happened. We watched it happen." It was geology in fast-forward.

Researchers often must endure difficult conditions to carry out their studies of glaciers. Here a group waits out yet another rain squall along the Variegated Glacier in Russell Fiord.

Following pages: In a final, dramatic plunge, a tower of ice ends its 76-mile journey down the Hubbard Glacier—longest valley glacier in North America—by calving into Disenchantment Bay.

Back on the Taku Glacier, Scott McGee, Susan Kaspari, and I set stake number 11, the final stake in Profile 2, and then weave our way back toward the safety of the Thiokol. Beneath our skis, the Taku moves slowly, inexorably, toward the sea.

Though the glacier moves like a living thing, the ice field itself can seem as lifeless as any place on the planet. Sitting on a ridge called Sunday Point and watching spotlights of sun illuminating the peaks one at a time, we look out over the unbroken white-on-white of ice more than 4,000 feet thick and see not a single living thing. Planes have fallen here, broken-winged, never to be found. Hikers and skiers have slipped, just that fast, into unseen cracks and vanished. There are places on this expanse where human voices have never been heard, where the silence is as old as ice. *(Continued on page 64)*

Wilderness guide Brock Tabor draws a map in the sand to depict the Hubbard Glacier's advances and retreats. In the future the glacier could flow across the mouth of Russell Fiord, but for now it calves into Disenchantment Bay. "It's like a parade," says Tabor. "When the glacier calves, we swing our heads around to watch; then we follow the bergs as they float by in the changing tide, putting on one of the greatest shows in the state."

A burst of Indian paintbrush and a fuzz of moss and lichen—early signs of life after a glacier's passing—gain a foothold on a slope near the Hubbard Glacier.

Following pages: Mendenhall Glacier creeps through the mountains just outside Juneau, Alaska's capital city. Easily accessible and with a recently expanded visitor center, the 12-mile-long Mendenhall is one of the state's most visited sites.

Pages 62-63: Icebergs sparkle in the waters of Glacier Bay National Park and Preserve. The Johns Hopkins Glacier (left background) calves so much ice that cruise ships can rarely approach nearer than two miles.

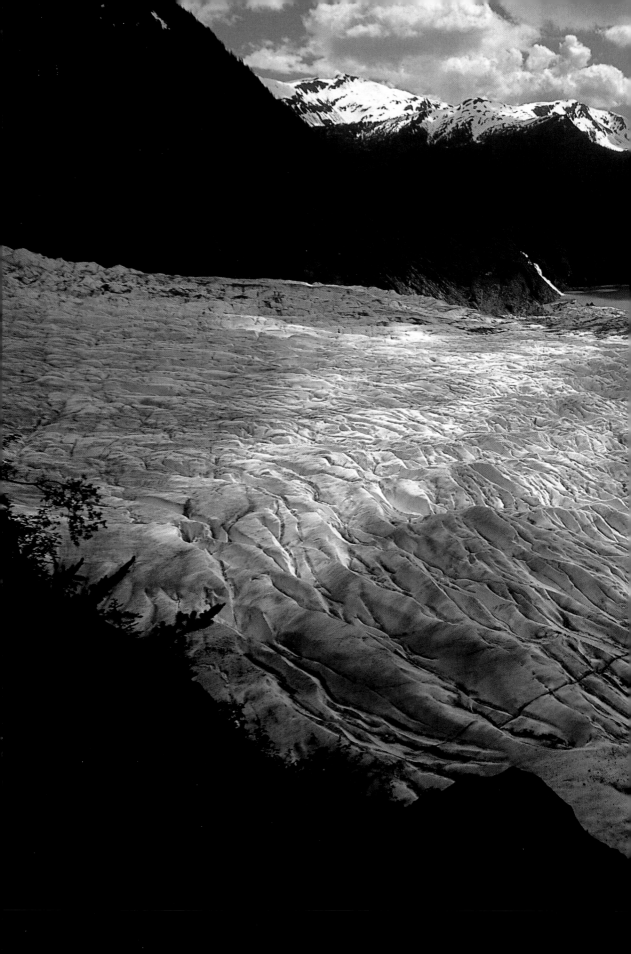

(*Continued from page 55*) Then a hummingbird zooms by; it is as colorful as a chip of a summer rainbow and just as unexpected. "We see them at Camp 10 once in a while, too," Scott says as the little bird vibrates the air around us with its wings, a blur at a hundred beats a second.

The ice, in fact, does support life: Red algae, when stepped on, turn footprints "bloody" and also tinge the air with the scent of watermelon; the springtail, a kind of snow flea, can jump a hundred times its length. Strange, almost mythical creatures called ice worms are not found on the Juneau Icefield, but they somehow thrive in places like Glacier Bay. Grizzlies, wolverines, Dall sheep, mountain goats, and lynx have been seen, too, using the flat surfaces of glaciers as highways through the peaks. An American black bear—the glacier bear—lives near the glaciers of Southeast Alaska; its coat is tinged silver and gray, as if the animal itself were slowly turning to ice.

On Sunday Point, the hummingbird zooms back one more time and then flits off, vanishing instantly against the immensity of the mountains and leaving us only the silence of the ice.

Even quieter is the bottom of a 16-foot-deep pit. "I am the only tenured ditchdigger in Alaska," physicist Toby Dittrich jokes a few days later as he and his crew excavate a pit in the ice of the Southwest Branch. "It's drudgery, but it is also some of the most important research we do." Like medical doctors taking tissue samples, he and his crew dig into glaciers to measure the depth and water content of each year's snowpack. "It's the 'annual mass budget' of the glacier. The higher the annual budget, the more likely the glacier will advance," he says, tossing out another shovelful of ice.

Besides reading scratch marks on rocks, Maynard Miller uses the survey results, annual mass budgets, and other data gathered over 50 years to paint a picture of the Juneau Icefield: "Thirty-seven of the thirty-eight glaciers that have their source on the ice field are losing the battle to atmospheric conditions. (Only the Taku is advancing.) That's not news. More than 90 percent of Alaska's glaciers are thinning and receding. What's news is that when we combine this data with similar data from glaciers in Patagonia, New Zealand, Norway, and elsewhere, we see this is a global phenomenon."

Miller says that "it is no longer a matter of proving whether the climate is warming; it is a matter of monitoring the effects of that warming and documenting how intense the changes are and how quickly they are occurring." To him, the subject is not an esoteric one: "This has enormously significant ramifications in natural history, human history, economics, agriculture, and even politics." Already scientists worry that massive calving off Columbia Glacier and others could endanger oil tankers in Prince William Sound.

In villages along the Arctic coast, the Inuit and Yupik who rely on walruses and seals are watching changing sea-ice patterns with concern. Ice loss could mean longer, more difficult travel and decreased hunting success. "I worry about the future," says Clifford Weyiouanna, a hunter from Shishmaref on the Seward Peninsula. "Will my children and grandchildren be able to hunt on the ice?"

What that future holds, no one can say. Some glaciers with broad, high-elevation source basins like the Taku could actually get "a kick in the pants," as Miller puts it, from warmer, wetter air and changing storm patterns. But we have more questions than answers. Like a giant crystal ball, the ice might hold at least a few of the answers. "Temperate glaciers, such as those of the Juneau Icefield, are some of the most sensitive indicators of climate change in the world," says Miller. "We see things first out here because we are not looking at outdated textbooks or computer models. We are looking directly at nature. The ice doesn't lie."

Back at Camp 10 after a day of field research, people are playing guitars, writing in their journals. There is the smell of wet wool drying. A turkey dinner slowly cooks in the propane-fired oven. "We have all the conveniences of a small city up here," Miller says. "But we have to work a bit for them, and that makes us appreciate them a little more." The opportunity to rest is also much appreciated. We have skied nine miles across the Western Hemisphere's fifth largest ice field today; dug a pit in the ice requiring, Toby Dittrich has calculated, energy equivalent to lifting a "ten-ton truck twelve feet in the air"; taken hours of measurements; then skied nine miles back to camp.

In the late sun, a group of students sit on rocks above the Taku Glacier, waiting for dinner; the sunshine is like gold coins on their cheeks. Watching them, I recall what Maynard Miller had said in a reflective moment: "When you sit out here on a high ridge, the ice field all around you, something strange happens. You feel both the minuteness of yourself and the shortness of life, but at the same time you have a sense of power as you look out to eternity and through the immensity of the world around you."

Can there really be a place so utterly barren and, at the same time, so staggeringly beautiful? Can this place stretching out below us truly be both an open book on the geologic past and a portent of our climate's future? Yes, I think to myself while resting on the ledge. Ice doesn't lie.

And then I think about fire. In June 1912, it seemed that hell had come to the North Pacific coast. Volcanic ash drifted down onto the streets of Seattle. In Vancouver, British Columbia, venomous rain disintegrated garments hanging on clotheslines. At Kodiak, thick ash caused birds to fall from the sky. Roofs collapsed. Ships couldn't dock in the harbor because of poor visibility. "A mountain has burst near here," Russian fisherman Ivan Orloff wrote to his wife in a letter from Kaflia Bay. "Night and day we light lamps. We cannot see the daylight…and we are expecting death at any moment…. Here are darkness and hell, thunder and noise…. Pray for us."

A new volcano—later named Novarupta—had burst to life near Mount Katmai. By some measurements, its three-day eruption was 30 times greater than the 1980 event at Mount St. Helens and more than twice the size of Mount Pinatubo's 1991 upheaval. The ash cloud reached Algeria by June 17 and almost circled the globe, cooling world temperatures by several degrees for the next year. Fisheries were devastated, water supplies were fouled, and crops wouldn't grow; yet not a single human life was lost.

In 1915 geologist Robert Griggs led a National Geographic expedition into the remote area to study revegetation in the volcanic zone. He returned to Katmai in 1916 and on July 31 topped a ridge from which he gazed upon the still smoldering source of all that "darkness and hell, thunder and noise."

"The sight that flashed into view as we surmounted the hillock was one of the most amazing visions ever beheld by mortal eye," he would later write. "The whole valley as far as the eye could reach was full of hundreds, no thousands—literally tens of thousands—of smokes curling up from its fissured floor."

Now part of Katmai National Park and Preserve, the Valley of Ten Thousand Smokes remains an amazing vision even today, a 40-square-mile moonscape where ash deposits as much as 700 feet thick buried the land. Just a few patches of fireweed soften the valley's edges almost a century after the eruption. Slivers of birdsong float above the sounds that silt-choked Knife Creek makes as it cuts a canyon through the compacted ash. It's like another planet here, so much so that Apollo astronauts have come to train for lunar missions. The valley no longer "smokes," but its silence and otherworldly beauty are stark reminders of the fire still burning in Alaska's heart.

In a 1,550-mile arc stretching from Mount Spurr west of Anchorage to Buldir Island in the western Aleutians, more than 40 active volcanoes ripple the landscape. "We usually have one or two pretty decent eruptions a year," says Chris Nye, a geologist with the Alaska Volcano Observatory (AVO). The AVO keeps an electronic finger on the pulse of 22 volcanoes and provides alerts and updates when one shows signs of rumbling to life. Even a partial list of eruptions over the past century can sound like cannon fire: Makushin, 7; Okmok, 11; Shishaldin, 18; Akutan, 20. Pavlof alone has erupted 29 times in the past hundred years. In 1986 it blew an ash cloud 10 miles into the air and caused dark snow to fall on nearby Cold Bay.

With the Kenai Peninsula on the east, the Chigmit Mountains on the west, and Anchorage at its north end, the Cook Inlet region is home to more than half the state's population and four major volcanoes: Spurr, Redoubt, Iliamna, and Augustine. "Those four are the ones that have the most immediate impact on Alaskans," says Nye. "As soon as they go off, they start dumping ash on the streets."

And go off they do. Augustine erupted in 1964, 1976, and 1986; Spurr in 1953 and 1992; Redoubt in 1933, 1966, and 1989-1990. The most recent

Redoubt event was a percussion of 23 eruptions that lasted five months and caused 100 million dollars in damage—the second-costliest volcanic incident in U.S. history, after Mount St. Helens. Ash clouds caused power outages and school closures. Heat from the blasts melted hundreds of millions of cubic feet of snow and ice, setting off major lahars—debris flows that threatened an oil-storage facility on the Drift River just north of the mountain; tanks at that facility were capable of holding 1.9 billion barrels of oil.

An eruption's effects, of course, are not limited to land and water. "Over 60,000 aircraft a year, more than 150 a day, fly above Alaskan volcanoes," says Chris Nye. "Anchorage is the number-one gateway for international freight in the country, so an event like the most recent one at Redoubt can be enormously disruptive to the airline industry." Or worse. On December 15, 1989, KLM Flight 867 from Amsterdam was unknowingly piloted into Redoubt's plume. Clogged with ash, all four engines stopped dead, and the plane began to fall from the sky over the Talkeetna Mountains. From an altitude of 27,900 feet, the 747 fell for five terrifying minutes, dropping nearly three miles before the crew managed to restart the engines and successfully land the crippled plane.

For decades after the 1912 eruption that created the Valley of Ten Thousand Smokes, the ground remained hot enough to melt researchers' shoes. Today, the 40-square-mile valley has cooled, yet life is only slowly returning to the ash-covered area.

For all its power and potential danger, a volcano is the epitome of mountain beauty, a swoop of stone and ash and earth that from a distance may appear as graceful as a sculpture. Picture Mount Edgecumbe rising over Sitka harbor, the sharp edge of Isanotski slicing the sky over Unimak Island, the perfect symmetry of Pavlof and its sister peak. "You also get gorgeous sunsets when they're going off," says Milt Holmes. He worked a sheep ranch on Unalaska Island's Chernofski Harbor for 41 years, a ranch surrounded by active Aleutian volcanoes.

"I remember riding home at night and watching Tulik sparking like fireworks," Holmes told me in his Unalaska home; he retired after his fifth hip operation finally got him off his horse. "Then there was the time my partner John and I were out riding and it started to snow—only it wasn't just snow; ash was falling, too. We put on goggles so we could see, and when we got back our faces were just black except for where our goggles (Continued on page 76)

Glaciers begin in clouds such as these near Reid Inlet in Glacier Bay National Park and Preserve. Over time, falling snow piles up in mountain recesses, and ever so slowly the weight of accumulating snow compacts lower layers into dense ice. When the ice becomes thick enough, it starts to move downhill like the Riggs Glacier (opposite), also in the park and preserve.

Following pages: With a sound the Tlingit people call "white thunder," the face of South Sawyer Glacier lets loose tons of ice into Tracy Arm.

Pages 72-73: An enormous cloud spawned by a weather system—and not by Mount Okmok below it—serves as a reminder that clouds of ash could someday erupt from this Umnak Island volcano.

Pages 74-75: Survivor of several eruptions by nearby volcanoes, the Cathedral of the Holy Ascension at Unalaska seems blessed by the sun lighting its face. This Russian Orthodox cathedral, one of the oldest churches in Alaska, dates from the mid-1890s and houses nearly 700 icons.

(Continued from page 67)   had been. I looked at John and started laughing until I realized he was laughing right back 'cause I looked just as silly as he did."

A 1987 earthquake measuring 6.4 on the Richter scale was not as funny. "It slammed into the house like a freight train," says Milt's wife Cora. "Sometimes I think we must've been crazy to voluntarily live between two live volcanoes."

"You grow up thinking the Earth is good and solid," adds Milt, "and then it tries to buck you right off. Something like that can change the way you think pretty quick."

One island down the chain from Milt Holmes's old sheep ranch is Umnak Island, home to Mount Okmok and the Bering Pacific Ranch. Rob Erixon, the 24-year-old ranch manager, has not yet experienced the full fury of Aleutian volcanoes the way that Milt and Cora Holmes have. He is pure cowboy: blond, blue-eyed, and straight off the Alberta prairie with a plug of chew beneath his lip and the round tattoo of a Skoal tin in the left hip pocket of his jeans. A cowboy in Alaska is not likely to admit being afraid of some old mountain.

When I ask him if he is concerned living for months at a time beneath an active volcano, he smiles. "Ah, it smokes and steams, but it's not like a bull or something."

Okmok's power, however, is apparent from the first step up Crater Creek. The bed of this creek is digging like a claw mark through a massive ashfall covering the island, and its banks are lined with uncountable house-size boulders, a toppled Stonehenge. "Must have been an amazing flood," says Jessica Faust Larsen, catching me staring at the creek from a ledge. A research assistant professor with the Geophysical Institute of the University of Alaska-Fairbanks, she is in her third field season at the volcano.

"Okmok is a bit of an anomaly," Jessica continues as I hike with her research team toward Okmok's rim. "It shows signs of several different kinds of eruptions. We want to know why this volcano emits massive, explosive pyroclastic flows, putting tons of ash up into the air and generating ash flows 20 meters thick, like the 2050 BP caldera-forming eruption. Usually Okmok erupts basalt, as evidenced by the thick one- to two-million-year-old deposits found as scattered outcrops about the island. When you get down to it, most of what we are trying to do with this research is answer three questions that are simple but amazingly complex," she says.

"Which are?" I ask.

"How and why and when."

Walking on a day with the lupine thick against our shins, chocolate lilies nodding in the breeze, and patches of buttercups as dense as snowdrifts, I have difficulty envisioning the kind of destruction Okmok has caused in the past. At least until I step to the rim of the caldera.

Rising more than 9,300 feet, Shishaldin Volcano (opposite) pokes through thick clouds covering Unimak Island in the Aleutians—longest chain of active volcanoes in the United States. On April 19, 1999, Shishaldin threw ash 45,000 feet into the sky.

As we climb up from the valley floor and leave the thick grass, our boots start to crunch on beads of black cinder where nothing grows. There are no wildflowers and no grasses—just burnt, black rock. Then the ground seems to open before me and I see Okmok Caldera, an immense wound in the Earth six miles in diameter. Within this ragged bowl of rock are a scattering of jewel green lakes and four separate cones, volcanoes within a volcano. Cone A, the most distant from where we stand, erupted basaltic material as recently as 1997 and is still steaming. Puffs of white drift lazily above it like twisted clouds.

Although currently quiet, this desolate and wildly beautiful caldera holds potential for devastating eruptions in the future. To stand on the rim is like watching a grizzly, too close, sleeping unaware in the grass. Or a bull.

The wind pummels us, ripping at the hoods of our jackets while we talk to each other and try to peer through the fog of so many years to see the volcano as it might have been. "Both the 2050 BP and the 8200 BP caldera-forming events were major, major eruptions," Jessica yells to me over the growl of the wind. "Each of them blew 20 cubic kilometers of material out of the crater, at a minimum. So much went out to sea that we have no way to measure it directly."

At the lip of Okmok Caldera, the author (right) talks with Jessica Faust Larsen and her research team from the Geophysical Institute at the University of Alaska-Fairbanks. They hope to unravel the secrets of this powerful volcano, which last erupted in February 1997.

In a calm moment between gusts, she looks out over the caldera and shakes her head slowly. "It would have been amazing to be able to sit and watch the volcano collapse into the caldera…and be able to survive it."

"Where might it be safe to watch such an eruption?" I ask.

Again Jessica shakes her head, thinking, and then laughs: "The space shuttle maybe."

We duck below the caldera's rim to get out of the wind before she continues: "If Okmok were to erupt today in an event like the 2050 BP caldera-forming eruption, it could have a severe impact on fisheries, a significant but short-term effect on climate, and a disruptive effect on airplane traffic."

"As a scientist, would you like to witness that in your lifetime?" I ask. This time she thinks a long while before answering.

"An event like that could have an enormous effect on people's lives, on the economy, the climate, and the environment, and it could potentially put a lot of lives at risk. So, as a human being, I don't want to see that happen. But I have to admit that from a purely scientific point of view it would be a great opportunity for research. With all the technology we have today, we could monitor the eruption, track the plume, watch how the environment responds." Her face brightens. "It would be an incredible thing to experience that in my lifetime."

For now, she takes it one rock at a time. The next day we hike along the cliff edge on Umnak Island's north side to look for outcroppings exposed by last winter's waves. "Wow! Look at that," says Jessica, pointing with her rock hammer to a layer of midnight black basalt hardened around a lighter brown ash-flow deposit along Ashishik Point. "Last year we were right here digging, looking for something like this, but we couldn't find it; this year, here it is. We'll have to take a sample back."

Satellites track the paths of volcanic plumes around the globe. Chemists analyze the "fingerprints" of ash, tracing the history of eruptions millions of years ago. Computers model the inner workings of subterranean volcanic plumbing. Yet even in an age of technology, a good part of the work of volcano research is still done by scientists down on their hands and knees in the dirt.

"People think that volcano research is all about fireworks and mountains blowing their tops," Jessica says during a rest, still kneeling in the sand. "It is exciting being on-site for an eruption or even monitoring the instruments back at the volcano observatory during a major event. But a lot of it, like the geochemical end of things, dating these samples, is more like putting a puzzle together—a lot less glamorous but no less important."

Watching Jessica hammering at the rock, and remembering Maynard Miller up on the Juneau Icefield struggling to get his students to see the stories written on the landscape, I think how simple research would be if we could just sit on a ridge, push a button, and view Earth's long history by fast-forwarding through geologic time. Glaciers would surge to slice mountains in half. Rivers would flicker like bolts of lightning to crack open canyons. Mountain ranges would bloom and shrivel as quickly as wildflowers, while the air all around was drumbeat with the sounds of erupting volcanoes. If we could see the world in geologic time, even for an instant, our sense of place would probably be forever shaken. We would never see a mountain or a wild-flower in quite the same way again. And perhaps all our questions would be answered in a flash.

Our lives, though, are too short for us to see Earth's history as anything but a snapshot. Kneeling in the sand at the cliff's edge, Jessica Faust Larsen cracks off a corner of the basaltic flow and drops it in a sample bag labeled OK-24B. It is one more small piece of the puzzle, another small step on the long path toward answers for three simple yet complex questions about Alaska's volcanoes: how and why and when. ▲

A ragged blanket of spring snow clings to Umnak Island's sleeping volcanoes, hugging the gentle slopes of a cone inside Okmok Caldera as well as the steep sides of Tulik Volcano, rising beyond the rim.

Twenty-four-year-old Rob Erixon, a Canadian cowboy, serves as sole caretaker for the Bering Pacific Ranch on Umnak Island. "After six weeks alone," he says, "I'm about ready to see people again."

Following pages: Augustine Volcano, about 180 miles southwest of Anchorage, remains one of Alaska's most active and potentially dangerous volcanoes. A 1986 eruption spewed ash on Anchorage streets, briefly stopped electricity, and temporarily closed the airport.

In the Kingdom of Space and Light

Even though I can see only a jumble of rock and ice below us, I know exactly where we are. So does Ed Hommer, sitting silently behind me. I glance again at the *X* on the map draped across my knees and wait to see if Ed will say anything as pilot Don Bowers banks our plane up Kahiltna Pass on the broad, icy shoulders of Mount McKinley.

The seconds drag on this May day in 2000. We are almost over the top. Just when I think the moment will pass without comment, Ed taps a finger against the cold window, pointing to the chaos of snow and ice below. "That's it, right there," he says. "That's where we went down."

Alaska is ribbed with mountains. Thirty-three distinct mountain ranges hold up the Alaskan sky—from the towering peaks of the Wrangells and the ice-jeweled Coast Mountains to rolling, lesser known ranges with names such as Bendeleben, Ray, and Romanzof. Thirteen of the highest peaks in the United States are here. Many more, their names and elevations not shown on maps, are simply remote, immense, and beautiful.

But no peak captures the soul as completely as Mount McKinley. On the streets of Talkeetna, you can see its effect: climbers fresh off the mountain, their sunburned faces still looking up. In Denali National Park and Preserve, you can see it in the eyes of people who have traveled from all over the world just to get a glimpse of the peak so often hidden in the clouds. "The mountain is out!" Word spreads quickly through the lodges and the campgrounds, on the tour buses, even in the streets of Fairbanks and Anchorage, where the peak looms on the distant horizon like the centerpiece of the world. "The mountain is out!" And all eyes turn to the sky.

Still, few people see Mount McKinley the way that Ed Hommer does. "The first time I saw it a shiver went up my spine," he says. "I was drawn to it. The desire to climb it has been a big part of my life ever since." Nearly 20 years would pass before he would make the attempt, and he would do so in a way no one could have imagined.

On a clear, windy December day in 1981, Hommer was piloting a flight-seeing trip out of Talkeetna to Mount McKinley via Kahiltna Pass. Mike

Clauser, Pat Scanlon, and Hommer's brother-in-law Dan Hartman were with him on the plane. Flying for an air service run by legendary pilot Cliff Hudson was a dream come true for Hommer, who grew up in the Midwest. "I was 26 years old, a bush pilot in Alaska. I had a wife, a baby on the way. Man, I thought I had the world by the tail."

That tail was about to give him a shake.

"We were heading up the pass," he says while staring out the plane window, remembering everything that had happened. "I saw a lenticular cloud hanging over the summit and was worried about the wind. So I radioed a plane coming down-glacier and asked how the ride was. He came back with 'just a slight bump.'"

Minutes later, "*Boom!* We got hammered." Hit by a violent downdraft, Hommer's plane was literally swatted out of the air. "It was as though someone had cut the cable to the elevator. *Bam!*"

"Everything went orange when we hit," he says of the crash. "Then I woke up in the snow with the plane's key still in my hand." One of the passengers was lying near the crumpled tail section. Ed Hommer stood up, took one step, and blacked out from the pain.

Crawling to the plane, he found his brother-in-law severely injured: "He was having trouble breathing…." Hommer's voice trails off, his eyes invisible behind the glacier glasses while emotions still swirl in him like crosswinds. "Anyway, we talked. I held him and he died in my arms. He was a good man."

The grim reality began to sink in—down in a small plane, one man dead and another, Pat Scanlon, gravely injured. The wreckage balanced precariously on a mountain where the wind can scream 100 miles an hour and drop the windchill factor to minus 100°F. They had no help and no way out, and darkness was setting in. With every passing hour their chances, like the Alaskan sky, grew dimmer and dimmer.

Late the next day, a helicopter managed to hover above the crash site. "I was thinking that we just might make it. They were so close I could see the crew chief waving at us." But landing on the steep slope was out of the question. Just holding steady in the same winds that had claimed Hommer's plane was nearly impossible. Low on fuel, low on daylight, the helicopter peeled off and disappeared. "I thought they'd be back," he tells me.

They were not coming back. Settling over the peak was a storm that would blow for five days straight, grounding all flights, burying the peak in veils of blowing snow, and leaving the survivors alone on the mountain.

"I thought things couldn't get any worse," Hommer says, but on the third day they did. A gust of wind caught the gnarled shell of the fuselage, used as a windbreak by the three survivors, and sent it careering down the mountain with the men still inside. "This is it, I figured. We're all dead now." The twisted metal slid, gaining speed, screeching in the snow, and heading for a cliff beyond which there was nothing but a thousand feet of cold, empty air. "This plane's going to fly one more time," he remembers thinking.

A paper birch belies the idea that Denali National Park and Preserve holds only rock, snow, and ice. Tundra, treeless hills, and forested valleys characterize Denali's northern half; peaks and glaciers dominate the south.

And then it stopped. The wing tip dug into the snow and the plane simply stopped. They were spared for the moment, but the jostling was too much for the critically injured Pat Scanlon, who died soon after. Also in the confusion, Hommer's boots had been ripped off and lost. His feet began to freeze.

For two more days the storm raged. Hommer and Mike Clauser clung to life on the side of the continent's highest peak, becoming hypothermic and dehydrated and beginning to hallucinate. "I saw my boss's wife on the glacier with a cup of coffee in her hand, as real as you could imagine," Hommer recalls. By sunset on the fifth day, time was running out: "We were down to hours. If they didn't get us that night, I knew for a fact that I was dead. I crawled out of the wreckage, sat in the snow, and picked out a view to die by."

What he saw was a figure running in the snow: "I thought I was having another hallucination, so I looked back down at my frozen feet." But the figure kept coming, and others followed. A group of local climbers, calling themselves the Mountain Maniacs, had braved the storm and miles of treacherous, crevasse-ridden glacier to hike and ski to the crash site. "It wasn't until they actually put their arms around me," Hommer says of the rescuers, "that I accepted the fact they were real."

The two men survived the mountain, but the battle was not over. Clauser would lose his fingers and toes. Hommer would suffer through a series of operations in a losing effort to save his feet. When the doctors finally gave him the grim news, he rebelled. "I was a climber, a pilot; I'd been active my whole life. How could I live without my feet?" Then, hours before the amputation, his wife gave birth to baby Carmen. "They wheeled her into my room," he says. "I took one look at that beautiful, perfect little girl and said to the doctors, 'Okay, I am ready now.'"

Ed Hommer lost both feet to above the ankles, and his life went into a tailspin. Unable to fly, he lost his job, too. He began to "turn midday beer drinking into a high art." Wracked with guilt and haunted by memories, he lost his appetite, dropped 40 pounds, and slumped into depression: "The airplane wasn't the only thing that crashed; my whole life crashed."

Following pages: **Pilot Keli Mahoney flies climbers to and from Mount McKinley. "People coming off the mountain are happy to head back but sad to leave," she says.**

Pages 92-93: **The summit of Mount McKinley remains irresistible decades after four Alaskans made the first ascent in 1913. Australian Damian Gildea, among nearly 12,000 climbers who have reached the top, did it alone in 2000.**

Finally, he hit bottom. "It just struck me one day, sitting there sipping my fifth beer around ten o'clock in the morning. I was on a down-bound train. I didn't like what I was becoming. Why did I survive if this was what I was going to let myself turn into?" He knew he had to turn things around. Eventually, Ed Hommer decided he had to climb the mountain that had almost killed him.

Our plane's skis skim the snow, coming to a stop as pilot Don Bowers announces, "Welcome to base camp." We have reached what climbers euphemistically call Kahiltna International, a flat spot on the Southeast Fork of the Kahiltna Glacier. Strung out across the snow, dozens of colorful tents bloom like vivid mushrooms. Skiers pull sleds piled with supplies. At an elevation of 7,200 feet, this camp is the staging area for climbers hoping to stand at the highest spot on the continent.

Each year around a thousand climbers attempt Mount McKinley. Only half reach the top; most are stopped by weather. "If we had perfect weather all season, 90 percent of the climbers would make the summit," says Denali's lead mountaineering ranger, Roger Robinson. "With the mountain's great height compared to its surroundings, McKinley acts as a huge barrier for storms. Minus 20°F or minus 30°F, with wind topping a hundred miles an hour, is not unusual high on the mountain. It can be unbelievably brutal." The combination takes a toll: Since 1932, 88 climbers have lost their lives on the peak, 11 in one year alone. Thirty-five bodies remain on the mountain.

"People thought I was coming back here to die," says Ed Hommer. "Actually, I was coming to find out how to live again. I was *(Continued on page 98)*

The two men survived the mountain, but the battle was not over. Clauser would lose his fingers and toes. Hommer would suffer through a series of operations in a losing effort to save his feet. When the doctors finally gave him the grim news, he rebelled. "I was a climber, a pilot; I'd been active my whole life. How could I live without my feet?" Then, hours before the amputation, his wife gave birth to baby Carmen. "They wheeled her into my room," he says. "I took one look at that beautiful, perfect little girl and said to the doctors, 'Okay, I am ready now.'"

Ed Hommer lost both feet to above the ankles, and his life went into a tailspin. Unable to fly, he lost his job, too. He began to "turn midday beer drinking into a high art." Wracked with guilt and haunted by memories, he lost his appetite, dropped 40 pounds, and slumped into depression: "The airplane wasn't the only thing that crashed; my whole life crashed."

Finally, he hit bottom. "It just struck me one day, sitting there sipping my fifth beer around ten o'clock in the morning. I was on a down-bound train. I didn't like what I was becoming. Why did I survive if this was what I was going to let myself turn into?" He knew he had to turn things around. Eventually, Ed Hommer decided he had to climb the mountain that had almost killed him.

Following pages: Pilot Keli Mahoney flies climbers to and from Mount McKinley. "People coming off the mountain are happy to head back but sad to leave," she says.

Pages 92-93: The summit of Mount McKinley remains irresistible decades after four Alaskans made the first ascent in 1913. Australian Damian Gildea, among nearly 12,000 climbers who have reached the top, did it alone in 2000.

Our plane's skis skim the snow, coming to a stop as pilot Don Bowers announces, "Welcome to base camp." We have reached what climbers euphemistically call Kahiltna International, a flat spot on the Southeast Fork of the Kahiltna Glacier. Strung out across the snow, dozens of colorful tents bloom like vivid mushrooms. Skiers pull sleds piled with supplies. At an elevation of 7,200 feet, this camp is the staging area for climbers hoping to stand at the highest spot on the continent.

Each year around a thousand climbers attempt Mount McKinley. Only half reach the top; most are stopped by weather. "If we had perfect weather all season, 90 percent of the climbers would make the summit," says Denali's lead mountaineering ranger, Roger Robinson. "With the mountain's great height compared to its surroundings, McKinley acts as a huge barrier for storms. Minus 20°F or minus 30°F, with wind topping a hundred miles an hour, is not unusual high on the mountain. It can be unbelievably brutal." The combination takes a toll: Since 1932, 88 climbers have lost their lives on the peak, 11 in one year alone. Thirty-five bodies remain on the mountain.

"People thought I was coming back here to die," says Ed Hommer. "Actually, I was coming to find out how to live again. I was *(Continued on page 98)*

"Ahhh...," says Stu Ramstad, enjoying a relaxing soak under the Alaskan sky. Looking back over the years, he remembers many changes while running the Little Mulchatna River Lodge on Fishtrap Lake in Lake Clark National Park and Preserve. But the beauty of the surrounding mountains endures, and a dip in the hot tub never seems to go out of style.

A handmade chair and a fixed-up cabin stand at Upper Twin Lake in Lake Clark National Park and Preserve. For nearly 30 years, Richard Proenneke stayed here—enjoying his own company and writing in his journal about living close to nature. The National Park Service plans to request historic site status for the cabin.

Following pages: Hikers pass a meltwater pond on the Root Glacier in Wrangell-St. Elias National Park and Preserve. Such ponds may seem innocuous, but their frigid waters make them danger spots for hikers.

(Continued from page 89) looking for closure. To find it, I had to go back to the crash site and climb beyond it—in both the spiritual and the physical sense."

Outfitted with specially designed artificial lower legs and accompanied by three other climbers, Ed Hommer set out from base camp on May 17, 1998, to confront two mountains: 20,320-foot Mount McKinley and an even higher, more personal one composed of fear, guilt, doubt, and difficult memories. Both summits proved too high. After 22 days on McKinley, the men found themselves pinned down by weather at 16,000 feet. "The wind sounded like a freight train," remembers Hommer. "You heard it coming with just enough time to dig your ice ax in and hang on." One other climber would die on the mountain in the same storm.

"At that point, I was asking myself just what the hell I was doing," Hommer says. "I had barely escaped being killed once before on the mountain, and now there I was again right in the teeth of it." Finally, with yet another storm moving in, they were forced to retreat, but not before Hommer visited the crash site. He left dried flower petals and a memorial to the two men who had lost their lives nearly 17 years earlier: "May your spirits dwell in high, beautiful places forever."

The next year, having made his peace at the crash site, Hommer tried a second time to reach the summit. He and climbing partner Kelly Raymond were again pinned down by wind, this time at 17,200 feet. For five days (ironically the same number Hommer had spent on the mountain after the crash), they shivered and waited. Then, he says, "I poked my head out of the tent at 10 a.m., and the air was perfectly calm. 'This is it!' I said to Kelly, and we took off."

At 7 p.m. on June 3, 1999, Ed Hommer became the first double-amputee climber with artificial legs to reach the top of Mount McKinley. "It started out as a very personal quest," he remembers, "but as I took the last few steps to the summit, I was thinking how important it was that someone with this kind of physical impairment was doing it—not that 'Ed Hommer' was going to be on the summit."

In August 2001, he and Kelly Raymond will begin another journey. They plan to climb Mount Everest from the north side, an ascent they hope will inspire others who have disabilities. "There might be some kid up against it like I was," Hommer says. "And looking at what Kelly and I are doing might give him that little extra shimmer of hope he needs to get through the day, then get up the next day and say he's going to try again."

As Don Bowers wings the plane away from the mountain through a slot known as One Shot Gap, Ed Hommer falls silent, watching Mount McKinley disappear behind him. "I'm a lucky man," he says softly. Lucky? Perhaps, but it takes more than luck to get you up the mountain.

(Postscript: On Monday, June 19, 2000, one month after this flight, veteran pilot Don Bowers crashed in the mountains near Mount McKinley. National Park Service

ranger Cale Shaffer and volunteer rangers Brian Reagan and Adam Kolff were with him on the plane. All four men died in the mountains that they loved.)

On a March night in 1987, the dogs begin to howl. I slip on my parka and boots and go outside the cabin to take a look around. This time of year, on the edge of the Brooks Range, the temperature dips to minus 30°F or below at night. The air is raw as I check each dog in turn—Whiteface, Royal, Rowdy, Yikes, 14 in all—their eyes reflecting red in the beam of my flashlight.

Nothing. Just a curl of smoke from the cabin chimney, the butter yellow light of a lantern glowing within. Something has them spooked; perhaps the wind carries the scent of caribou or brings the far-off sounds of wolves. Then I glance up: The sky is on fire with the northern lights, the aurora borealis. I walk to the river to be out from under the trees.

In northern Alaska, almost every dark night brings the chance to witness the aurora. More than 200 times a year, the sky swells and sways with ribbons of light—soft green, ghostly white, and a red that pulses as if someone is blowing across the embers of a campfire.

The displays once were a mystery, the stuff of lore and legend. Then 20th-century scientists provided an explanation for the origin of the northern lights: an electromagnetic reaction spawned by enormous solar flares interacting with Earth's atmosphere. But researchers still don't understand all of the aurora's effects. The University of Alaska-Fairbanks facility at Poker Flat, for example, is looking into how bursts of auroral activity disrupt satellite communications and may even lead to corrosion in the trans-Alaskan pipeline.

On a night like this, I wonder just how much we really want to know about the aurora. The fact that some questions are still unanswered reaffirms what many of us want to believe about nature: Things exist beyond the weights and measures of scientific inquiry; the universe is made up of more than quantifiable biomass. Mystery has its place, and perhaps that place is in the darkness of an Arctic night, on the banks of a frozen river where I am standing alone beneath a sky dancing with light, my neck bowed backward.

Finally the dogs are quiet, curled like fists against the cold. The moon has risen, dimming the aurora. In the moonlight the high peaks of the Brooks Range glow blue-white, still a day's travel north by dogsled. Tomorrow we will harness the dogs and push deeper into the range. But that's for tomorrow. For now I blow out the lantern and slip back into my bunk. The warm, dark cabin is filled with the smells of wet wool, lantern smoke, and bubbling chili. All night there are lights flickering in my dreams.

"Are you set?" David Ketscher asks me in the morning. He owns Sourdough Outfitters, a guiding company in the tiny village of Bettles north of the Arctic Circle. The two of us will mush up the frozen back of the North Fork of the Koyukuk River in the Brooks Range to set camps that Ketscher later will use on ten-day dogsledding trips with clients. A big, barrel-chested man with biceps that are as large as my legs, he has a surprisingly gentle and mischievous spirit, laughing for hours about slipping a rubber worm in my chili bowl or harnessing eight spirited dogs to my nearly empty sled just to watch the ride.

"Ready," I answer naively. The dogs yelp and howl, leap and twirl, tangling their leads. It is chaos—furred, fanged, four-legged chaos.

"Reach down, undo the anchor, step off the brake, and yell 'Hup!'" he shouts over the wild barking. "And…oh yeah…hang on!"

Big dreams and big horizons continue luring people to Alaska. Only hardy folks such as Trapper and Marilyn Austin—photographed on one of their trips into Eagle—stay and make their homes here.

As if shot out of a cannon, the dogs lunge forward in unison, nearly sending the sled airborne. The dark lines of the spruce trees flash by, blurred with speed. I hear a screeching sound, which doesn't stop until I realize I am still standing on the claw brake and let up. This action only makes me go faster, the wind ripping tears out of my eyes.

Just when I think I might career wildly into the void, everything goes white. We shoot out of the tunnel of trees into the blinding light of the frozen river. The dogs go silent, falling into a traveling pace; their harnesses jingle like sleigh bells. As I take my first breath, David is wrenched around on his sled, laughing. A long time passes before I gather the courage to turn my head and look at the country we are traveling through.

The Brooks Range is the northernmost mountain range in the United States. In a 700-mile arc it sweeps across Alaska, separating the vast interior from the coastal plains and tundra of the far north. The nearly 20-million-acre Arctic National Wildlife Refuge protects the eastern part of the range while the central section, where we are, lies within the 8.4-million-acre Gates of the Arctic National Park and Preserve. It is a trailless, roadless wilderness —"a black belt park" as one Park Service planner called it—and it is as wild as Alaska gets.

On this morning the peaks are diamond bright, white-on-white in endless rows, deep blue where the wind has scoured the snow off the rock. The land seems empty, but our sleds cross animal trails: hip-deep moose tracks in the willows, the arrow-straight trail of lynx, the outline of what looks like an angel's wing where a ptarmigan has taken flight.

A few hours upriver we cut the trail of a Dall sheep, alone and vulnerable in the valley bottom. A bit farther, from both sides, come the star-shaped tracks of three—perhaps five—wolves; the exact number is difficult to make out in the constellation of tracks, directly in line with those of the sheep. What will happen to that sheep is written as surely in those tracks as if in stone: First we see a few tufts of white hair, then splatters of blood on the snow. We round a bend to find the partially frozen carcass of a full-curl Dall sheep, its legs bent as though trying to run even in death. In the brush are wolf eyes, watching and waiting.

We will be five days on the trail, with David keeping a hard pace and rarely stopping to rest. So I am surprised when I see him pulled up just ahead. As my sled catches up with his, David points to a mountain pass. "A valley's up there somewhere," he says, his mustache striped with ice. "It has a name that means something like 'place of perfect beauty.'" With that, he clucks to his team and moves off, leaving me to watch the pass vanish in a curtain of blowing snow. Even as it does, I know where I am going someday.

T welve years later, I step off a plane at the Nunamiut village of Anaktuvuk Pass with Carol Kasza, a longtime friend and wilderness guide. This time the season is high summer. Songbirds whistle from the tundra. The peaks ringing the valley blush with fireweed as if they are embarrassed at their own lush beauty. Our plan is to set off on a two-week hike and paddle through the heart of Gates of the Arctic National Park and Preserve, seeking the Place of Perfect Beauty.

I could have checked the maps or asked a ranger, but I don't want the search to be that easy. In too many places, guidebooks and interpretive displays have rubbed the sense of discovery right out of our national parks. This time I want to be successful, or not, on my own. I want to be surprised.

We shoulder our packs and hike the gravel road to the edge of town. The village of Anaktuvuk Pass was settled just 50 years ago as the permanent home of the Nunamiut, the last seminomadic culture on this continent. Its name means "place of caribou dung," and the location was chosen for one reason: caribou. Twice a year, spring and fall, as many as 500,000 caribou stream through the central Brooks Range—a snorting, trotting, kicking river of life.

"We need the caribou," says Lela Ahgook, a Nunamiut woman we meet camped with her husband, Noah, a few miles out of town. A cloud of mosquitoes has come up while we talk, making us brush our hands in front of our faces as if we are constantly waving hello…goodbye…hello. Noah, the hunter, scans the horizon and slips another (Continued on page 112)

Tired but not defeated, Dick Griffith crosses a stream near McCarthy at the end of the five-day, 150-mile Alaskan Mountain Wilderness Race. The 2000 event, held in Wrangell-St. Elias National Park and Preserve, marked Griffith's 19th long-distance wilderness race. "They are tough," says the 73-year-old Griffith, "but I always manage to finish."

Opposite: Wrangell-St. Elias National Park and Preserve offers 13 million acres of possibilities for visitors who want to climb mountains or descend into the blue jaws of glaciers. "You can do wonderful, beautiful climbs up here," says guide Bob Jacobs, "that no one outside of the climbing world ever heard of."

Following pages: In the Chugach Mountains, light, snow, rock, and distance create memorable vistas for horizon-gazers. Here, slopes near Palmer seem to glow from within.

Pages 106-107: East of Anchorage, snow-dusted Chugach summits ascend to the clouds.

Pages 108-109: Sharp peaks outside of Palmer take on a reddish hue as sunlight temporarily transforms them.

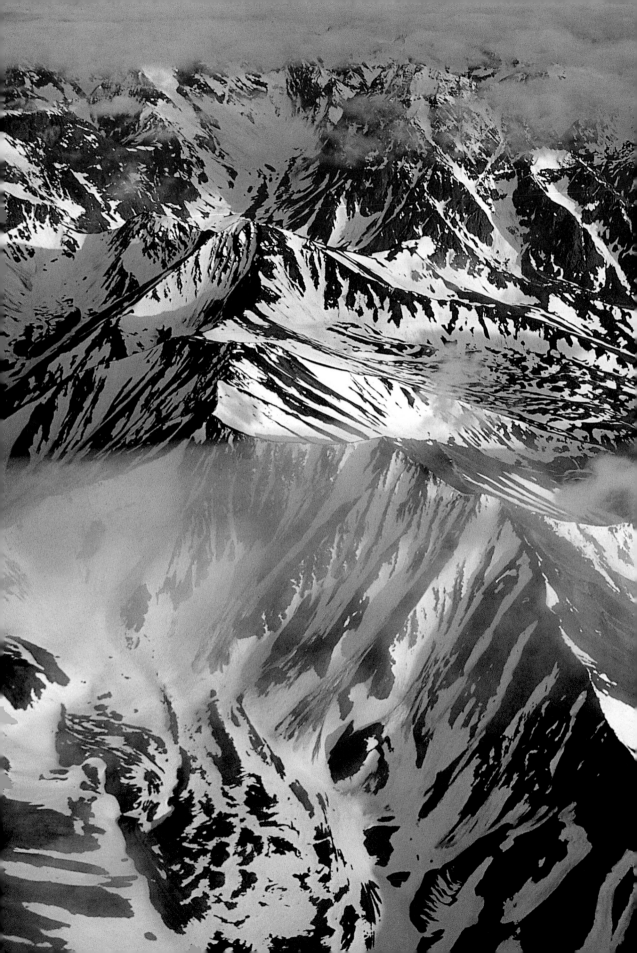

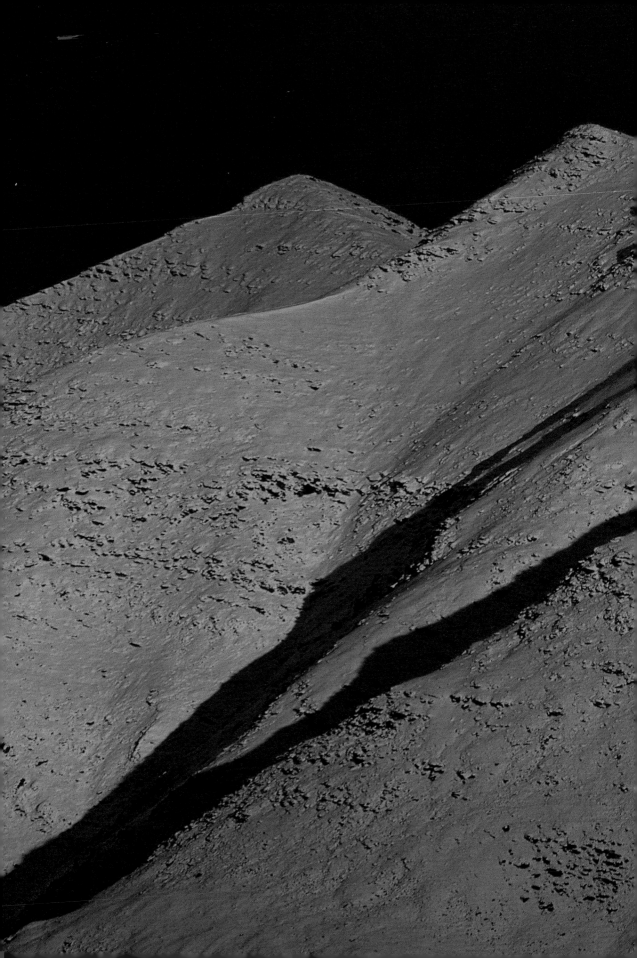

Everything from groceries and mail to the occasional visitor arrives by floatplane (left) at the Takahula Lake home of Steve and Kay Grubis (above), basking in the autumn sunlight with their dog Monk. The only residents of the 8.4-million-acre Gates of the Arctic National Park and Preserve, they have for the last 15 years carved a life from both the dreams and the reality of the Alaskan bush.

(*Continued from page 101*) cigarette into the gap where his front teeth used to be. Lela does the talking: "In spring the hunting was not good, so now people in the village don't have enough meat." Noah nods, slipping in another cigarette.

"Do you know the name of that canyon?" I ask, pointing to a cut of gold-brown rock that ends in a dizzying rise to a peak.

"Amaguayaat," Lela says, "place where the wolf has pups." As we hike away, I notice wolf tracks in the mud.

"Look at those peaks," I say to Carol miles later, still thinking about names. "In the lower 48 they'd have their pictures on coffee mugs and post-cards. There'd be a scenic turnout and a visitor center. Here they don't even have names," I say, slapping the map.

Announcing autumn's touch, bearberry blazes scarlet on the tundra in Denali National Park and Preserve. This member of the heath family thrives in open areas as well as in rocky or sandy woodlands.

"I know," she says, smiling. "Isn't it great? In other places you have pockets of wilderness, but in the Brooks Range we still have the whole, intact ecosystem. It is a gift I hope we have the wisdom to preserve." As if in a grace note to that thought, a grizzly walks through camp that night—blond as dry grass, its belly dark from crossing the creek. Walking with the confidence of a king, the animal reaches a ridge and, backlit, disappears into the nameless mountains.

Next morning we wake to rain. Clouds hang like gray skirts, revealing only the knobby knees of the mountains. For days we walk through air so heavy it makes us feel as if we are carrying the sky. Locked beneath my raincoat, I wonder with every step if I am walking right past the Place of Perfect Beauty, hidden by the fog. Carol, who has spent 20 years guiding in the Arctic, senses my frustration. "You have to accept this land as it is," she tells me as we duck behind a boulder and out of the wind. "The bugs, the rain, the beauty. The land is what it is, not what we might want it to be. When you accept that, wonderful things can happen."

One of those "wonderful things" happens as we are hiking up a long ridge a little before midnight. At first the sky is thick with clouds; the next moment it is clear and pastel blue. The light goes rich gold on the grass, brilliant white on the tufts of cotton grass that fringe a tiny lake. This far north the sun doesn't set between May and August, spinning low around the sky like a red ball spun above a child's head. In the soft sunlight, the land looks painted in oils, blessed with beauty.

"Ahhh," Carol says as we walk bathed in the glow of the midnight sun. "To me, this is perfect beauty." She closes her eyes, tilts back her head, and spins in slow circles while cupping her hands and letting the sunlight pour over her. But the moment doesn't last long, and the rain returns.

We hike on through a land that seems bent on keeping its secrets, the door to every valley slammed shut by a wall of gray fog. For three days we camp on the banks of the North Fork of the Koyukuk, waiting for the storm-swollen river to recede before crossing to our raft on the other side. All the while, I wonder what lies within those canyons hidden in the fog.

"So, Jeff, do you think you found it?" Carol asks days later as we drift downstream on the same river David and I had followed years before on sleds.

"Not a specific place I can point to on a map," I answer gloomily.

"Sometimes people get hung up on labels," she says. "It's like calling this a 'national park' and what is just east of here a 'national wildlife refuge.' It's all really just the Brooks Range. We need to learn to see things as a whole if we ever hope to understand or protect them. The names on a map don't matter to the mountains."

Perhaps she's right. Downstream, through a break in the fog, a mountain peak appears from inside a cloud as if behind frosted glass. My first thought is to grab the map and look up the name. But I don't do it. Instead, I set the map down and just look. Beauty isn't found on a map. It is wherever you find it, and at this moment beauty is in a wild, nameless mountain suddenly unwrapping itself from the fog.

Wrangell-St. Elias National Park and Preserve is a kingdom of peaks where four major ranges converge: the Wrangells, the Chugach, the St. Elias, and the Alaska Range. Peaks rise like exclamation points from sea level to more than three miles high. Nine of the thirteen highest peaks in the United States are found here, and more summits top 14,500 feet than anywhere else on the continent.

This is a kingdom of space. Wrangell-St. Elias is the country's largest national park, with 13.2 million acres and glaciers that are as large as small eastern states. Yellowstone, by comparison, is only one-sixth the size.

It is also a strange place to hear a horn. Nevertheless, Cliff Wright is just now honking an old-fashioned, rubber-ended, curlicue bulb horn from his porch, directing me by sound through the maze of swamp and forest that surrounds his isolated cabin. I have come here to explore something Cliff knows a great deal about: solitude, another treasure of Alaska's mountains.

As much as gold or oil, herds of caribou or nets of fish, the opportunity for a person to spend time truly and utterly alone is one of the state's great natural resources. Alaska has a long history of solitude seekers. Jim Huscroft lived alone for years on Cenotaph Island on Glacier Bay's outer coast. He read a stack of year-old newspapers one day at a time and baked 14 different kinds of pies for himself at Christmas. Richard Proenneke's cabin in Lake Clark National Park and Preserve was not only his home but also a work of art.

Whether it's a life as a hermit or a two-week canoe trip without seeing another human being, solitude is a treasure, and Cliff Wright is a man who can tell me about it. Since 1966 he has lived in an 18-by-16-foot, one-room, six-windowed cabin along Dan Creek, first with his wife and son, then alone when they left in 1980. At 63, he is a sprite of a man, barely five feet five inches tall; his waist is so narrow that his black belt nearly circles him twice. Cliff is neatly dressed, with a plaid shirt covering his turtleneck sweater, and he wears eyeglasses that are perhaps too large for his face.

"Sorry about being scruffy. I'm about three days behind in trimmin' up," he says, rubbing his chin. "I wasn't expecting company." Still, he invites me inside. His last visitors—hikers who stumbled upon his cabin—arrived in June, and their dirty dishes remain in the sink even though we are now in mid-August. "Shows you how often I do dishes, huh?"

The cabin is crowded but tidy: Stacks of books and magazines fill every shelf; a picture of trumpeter swans, painted by his wife, hangs over the elevated bed. A Ruth Washington woodstove, thirdhand, commands one wall. There are two chairs and a sawed-off tree stump he uses for a footrest. A vase full of pussy willows sits on the windowsill. A JC Higgins single-shot shotgun over the door is loaded with bird shot, ready to pepper the backsides of bears that get too friendly. "I don't want to hurt them, but they keep crawling up on my front porch."

Not accustomed to having company, Cliff talks slowly at first, often closing his eyes as if trying to maintain the solitude. He quickly warms up, however, and for the next five hours he talks a swift river. Stepping in to interrupt would not be a good idea, I think.

Growing up in Florida, Cliff dreamed of a life in Alaska. With a degree in marine ecology from the University of Florida at Tampa, he came north in 1965 on a temporary fisheries job. A year later, he got a free ride back to the state by delivering a brand-new Chevy El Camino ("I think it was stolen") to a buyer in Anchorage. He remembers seeing this landscape in September, "the primo time of year," and thinking that Alaska was everything he ever pictured it would be. So, he started building his cabin.

Since that time, Cliff has gotten by on the $1,500 to $2,000 a year he earns doing odd jobs that he picks up now and then. He cuts wood by hand, hauls water from the creek, and every few months takes a long walk back to civilization, where he gets his mail and buys supplies. Groceries are carried in on his back 25 to 35 pounds at a time. He makes jewelry, listens to the radio, and writes long poems in the meter and rhyme of Robert Service:

I know I must go to those pastures of snow
To savor their deep kind of living.
Where life is direct, it makes you reflect
How nature is so unforgiving.

Cliff leads a quiet life, making notes on his wall calendar to track the days: April 7, "Trumpeter Swans return"; April 13, "First mosquito, packed in groceries"; April 19, "Biking on frozen pond, fell once, wasn't hurt, lots of fun."

"I am lazy by nature," he admits when I point out the number of blank spaces on the calendar. "Once I got out of the Air Force I said to hell with regimentation, including my own. I slump into the habit of staying up late, 2 a.m. or later, listening to the radio or reading, and then I sleep a few hours, get up, make a cup of coffee, and go back to sleep for a few more hours."

"What attracted you to this kind of life?" I ask between poetry readings.

"Freedom from and freedom to," he says. "Freedom from noise, pollution, the whole rat race, and freedom to enjoy the beauty and the solitude." That solitude has had a price, though. Cliff talks often of "getting a honey" and tells me about the letters he's written to the ads in the backs of magazines: "Russian Women Want to Meet American Men." He's gotten responses but hasn't taken things further. He writes long letters to friends, dreams of a bike trip from Alaska to South America, and corresponds with his "adopted daughter," an Ecuadoran child whom he sponsors.

Following pages: One of the six designated Wild and Scenic Rivers within Gates of the Arctic National Park and Preserve, the blue Alatna meanders across the landscape, following a path as twisted as thread trailing from a dropped spool.

Still, loneliness lies close to the surface. Outside, we spot a pair of trumpeter swans, white as angels, which have been returning to this same pond for as long as Cliff has lived here. "Did you know they mate for life?" he asks several times during the few minutes we sit watching.

This life of solitude and silence is not for everyone. Yet, as we hike back to where I will meet the pilot, Cliff scoots ahead to point out edible plants, circles in the grass where bears have made day beds, and willows where beavers have been at work. His familiarity with the landscape is the kind that only years of looking closely can bring. Before very long, perhaps no living person will know what it means to dwell in the wilderness. A person can't just walk into a national park and put up a cabin any more. Who will know what it means to go a whole winter without hearing another human voice? Who will mark the return of the swans in spring?

Once, Cliff stops so suddenly on the trail I nearly bump into him. Looking me in the eye, he says, "You know, if I were to kick off tomorrow, I would have lived my dream out here." How many of us can say that about our own lives? I wonder. But there is no time to answer. I have to run to catch up with Cliff, who is already ten steps down the trail and still talking up a storm. ▲

"No one knows the way of the wind or of the caribou," the Gwich'in people say. Photographer Michael Melford learned firsthand about the unpredictable spirit of both: "Our first morning at this camp in a lovely little valley of the Brooks Range, we woke to snow and plenty of caribou. By sunset, the snow had melted and the caribou were gone."

A bleached caribou antler marks the yearly passage of hundreds of thousands of caribou through Gates of the Arctic National Park and Preserve.

Opposite: Slow-moving ice from the Bagley Icefield left behind this stray boulder, known as a glacial erratic.

Following pages: Like waves gone to stone, the crests of the Arrigetch Peaks in the Brooks Range form a sea of snow-dusted mountains.

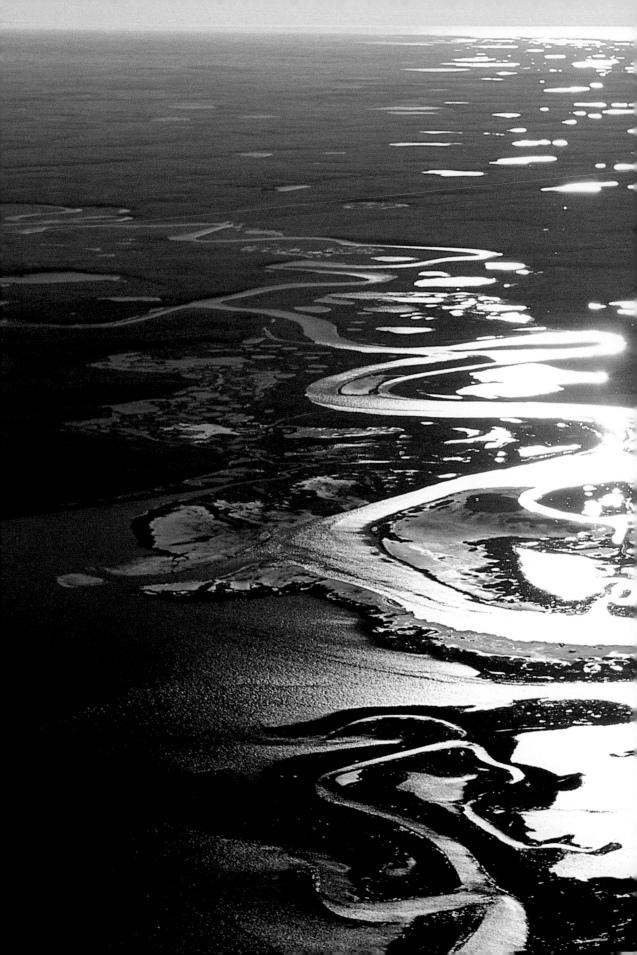

CHAPTER 4

Through the Mists of Time

In the far north, the sun never leaves the sky in summer and it doesn't rise in winter. In the waters off the west coast, Yupik whale hunters drift back and forth across the International Date Line, from "today" into "tomorrow." Time moves differently in Alaska, or so it seems, particularly on soft gray days when fog and mist shroud the tor-lined ridges of the Serpentine River Valley in Bering Land Bridge National Preserve.

Artifacts from this valley indicate humans were here at least 6,000 years ago. But for perhaps even longer, people have been coming to this place to heal, to pray, and to soak in the hot, mineral-rich waters that bubble up from the very soul of the Earth. Shamans have come to touch the spirit world. Miners, hikers, and people of coastal villages have come to ease the aches of hard work, long hikes, and cold winters.

At Serpentine Hot Springs you can still find beauty, sacredness, and power. This is a spot where on a foggy day even time itself seems to get tangled in the mist. Just ease down into a 140°F, jade green pool and let the rising mist blur your sense of time. Squint your eyes: You might be able to see an early winter day hundreds of centuries ago. Perhaps a bull steppe bison grazes in the green-brown swell of a small river valley. Perhaps a ray of low sunlight, almost without warmth, touches the top of a distant ridge. The bison looks up once, stops chewing, and bows its head to graze. Before its gray-black muzzle touches the wind-bent grasses there is a rustling in the brush, followed by a blur of teeth and claws and dust. A sound between a groan and a bellow gurgles from the bison's throat, and then—36,000 years later—the phone rings in Dale Guthrie's office at the University of Alaska in Fairbanks.

"We received a call from a miner, in July 1997, saying a couple of hooves were sticking out of a silt bank he was working near Fairbanks," Guthrie (now professor emeritus) tells me at the University of Alaska Museum. "Although we get reports about mummies all the time, good specimens are exceptionally rare…about one a decade all across the Arctic. In Alaska it has happened maybe five or six times in the last century. This one, however, turned out to be pretty spectacular."

Fossils and bones provide clues to a creature's anatomy, but a nearly intact mummy of a Pleistocene steppe bison was a scientific bonanza allowing scientists to ask a broader range of questions. Hair samples gave clues to environmental trace elements. Complete muscle masses helped flesh out a detailed picture of body shape. Plant fragments trapped among the teeth told of the bison's diet and revealed what plant types thrived in Alaska so long ago.

Still, there were mysteries. Early in Guthrie's research on the bison that he dubbed "Blue Babe," he hypothesized that the animal had died from natural causes and been scavenged by smaller creatures. But scratches and punctures on the carcass nagged at his mind: "I thought, just as a kind of fantasy on the way home one evening, Wouldn't it be interesting if those scratches were lion marks?" Returning to the lab, he took the skull of an American lion, a predator that once roamed Alaska and was not unlike modern-day African lions, and placed its large incisor teeth against marks on the mummy.

They were a perfect match. In the hide, a tooth fragment—part of a lion's carnassial—confirmed the theory: Blue Babe had been killed by two, possibly three, American lions. "The story started to get better and better," says Guthrie. "Instead of just a description of the carcass, we had evidence of how the bison died and what the ecological picture could have been in northern Alaska 36,000 years ago."

That picture shows a very different northern Alaska, drier and colder than it is today. Prowling the land were beavers the size of black bears, as well as camels, woolly mammoths, and short-faced bears that could reach higher than a basketball hoop when they stood on their hind legs. "The whole of the north, from Alaska to England, would have been a vast grassland for which there is no good surviving counterpart today," Guthrie says. The region was treeless and windswept, with tangles of brush in the river valleys. "Blue Babe was killed probably in one of those valleys," Guthrie theorizes, "because that's where there was good cover for lions, which had to get fairly close before they made a run."

Today, Blue Babe rests in a glass case in the University of Alaska Museum, forever caught in the death pose it struck as the lions brought the bison to its knees. The discovery proved to be "a set piece in constructing the way we view the Pleistocene," Guthrie says. "It was a book thrown through time."

But before he could close the covers on that book, Guthrie wanted to learn one more thing: "I'd grown up hearing about Russian hunters eating steaks from frozen mammoths in the Arctic. No scientist had ever before had the opportunity to prove or disprove these stories." So, he and his wife scraped a few morsels of red meat from the still frozen bison carcass, gathered a group of brave friends and colleagues, and with a "good bottle of burgundy" sat down to a meal of 36,000-year-old steppe bison stew. Dale Guthrie is a man who now knows what time tastes like. "It tastes," he says with a smile, "a little muddy."

At Serpentine Hot Springs, your eyes begin to make out something else in the mist rising around you. Perhaps you can see a face—an ancient, timeless face—the kind that Anchorage artist L. Saunders McNeill sees when she looks through her lens to compose a portrait of Tiggerrahmii, a Siberian Yupik woman on the Chukchi Peninsula of the Russian Far East.

Click! The camera shutter snaps in the dim, dusty silence of the tiny home set at the edge of the Bering Strait. On the old woman's face, decorated with the long, dark marks of traditional tattooing, are the deep-set creases and lines of a life that has been spent in a harsh place, and yet Tiggerrahmii's eyes are strong and wise.

Soon McNeill will return to Alaska, stopping at villages like Savoonga and Gambell on St. Lawrence Island to photograph the Yupik elders on the Alaskan side of the Bering Sea. In those faces she will see the same deeply etched lines and creases, the same wisdom of lives spent close to the land. And she will see a bridge. "It can be difficult," she says, "to look at the 50 miles or so of water separating Alaska from Siberia and realize that the two were connected by a land bridge. I think it is an easier concept to visualize when you can see the faces."

At least ten times in the past 800,000 years, lower sea levels exposed fingers of land reaching out from Alaska and Siberia to form what is now known as Beringia. Sometimes a land bridge a thousand miles wide extended from the Aleutian Islands north to beyond Barrow, connecting the two great continents. One long-held theory says that humans from Asia first came to North America over that land. *(Continued on page 138)*

Opposite: Hundreds of tiny, shimmering lakes dot beach ridges in Bering Land Bridge National Preserve.

Following pages: Long an important route between the interior of northwest Alaska and the coast, the Noatak River bears an Inupiat name meaning "from deep within."

Pages 132-33: Great Kobuk Sand Dunes cover 25 square miles in northwest Alaska. Artifacts dating from about 10,000 years ago show that hunters passed through this region during the Ice Age.

Smiles in the summer sun: A group of local kids enjoy a tug-of-war contest on St. Paul, one of the Pribilof Islands in the Bering Sea. Part of the Independence Day celebration, this yearly competition pits the men against the women.

Outpost of patriotism, St. Paul Island celebrates the Fourth of July with a flag-waving Uncle Sam and a parade along the hilly streets (above). The holiday's other festivities include a greased pole climb, a pie-eating contest, and the popular tug-of-war.

Bounty of the Newhalen River, slabs of sockeye salmon hang on wooden racks to dry. The Newhalen flows into Iliamna Lake, from which as many as 60 million salmon make their way each spring to the Kvichak River and eventually Bristol Bay. They return one to four years later to spawn, completing a cycle as old as Alaska itself.

Fur seals pepper the beaches of St. Paul Island in the
Pribilofs. Each July the female seals head for shore to
give birth. Soon after, the males arrive and battle to
form harems for the breeding season, which will start
the whole cycle again.

(Continued from page 129) "People call Alaska the Last Frontier," says Bob Gerhard of the National Park Service in Anchorage, "but I like to think of it as the First Frontier as well." Nomadic hunters could have crossed Beringia into coastal Alaska more than 30,000 years ago or, as some scientists theorize, only as recently as 15,000 years ago; they may have followed the herds, moving east and south along glacier-free corridors. New research also points to the possibility of early migrants coming by boat, hugging the shoreline.

By 11,000 years ago, the sea covered the land bridge again. Yet even after the land was submerged, more people—ancestors of the Inupiat, the Aleut, and the Yupik—came to coastal Alaska. Then, as today, about 50 miles of the Bering Strait separated mainland Alaska from Siberia. Although cold and stormy, this body of water is still not an impassable barrier to animals or humans. The two sides are knit together by cranes, geese, swans, and songbirds that fly across the strait to feed and nest. Marine mammals such as walruses, whales, and seals travel the waters freely.

For generations, so did the Siberian Yupik. About half the Yupik live on the Alaskan coast, the others on Russia's Chukchi Peninsula. Hunters and families once regularly crossed the strait in small boats. They were part of one culture, with an ocean strait between them. Then, in the 1940s, politics did what miles of windswept waters could not. The Cold War between the United States and the Soviet Union closed the border, effectively raising an "Ice Curtain" across the strait, a barrier that would stand for more than 40 years.

"For four decades, they were cut off, cousins from cousins, friends from friends," says L. Saunders McNeill. Finally, in the late 1980s, tensions eased and the Ice Curtain began to melt. McNeill set out to compose a portrait of every living Yupik elder on both sides of the Bering Strait, "to put a face on the forcibly divided families." Her portraits often have provided the first photographic evidence of relatives who haven't seen each other in decades. "I show a photograph and the people just light up," she says. "Elders sometimes caress the photograph; small children who've been told of their relatives will kiss it as if the person were really in front of them."

Improving relations between the U.S. and the U.S.S.R. brought more signs of cooperation. A Soviet icebreaker was sent to help when gray whales were trapped by ice near Barrow in October 1988. Later, another Soviet ship brought people and supplies to aid in the cleanup of the *Exxon Valdez* oil spill.

There is talk of establishing a Beringian Heritage International Park that would encompass both sides of the strait and commemorate the links between the peoples and lands of the two countries. The U.S. has already designated Bering Land Bridge National Preserve, Cape Krusenstern National Monument, Noatak National Preserve, and Kobuk Valley National Park, all of which could become part of the international park, but worsening economic and political conditions in the former Soviet Union have held up plans across the strait. "Conditions over there are horrifying," says McNeill. "They have no coal, no electricity, no running water. The people are more concerned about finding food or getting fuel for the winter than they are about a park right now."

Such conditions can be hard to witness. "A Siberian woman came to visit us with her nine kids," says Alma Toolie, a Yupik from Savoonga. "The kids didn't want to leave. We gave them tennis shoes, shirts, jackets, whatever we could, but still they cried and cried. It touched my heart real bad," she says with tears in her own eyes. "I told them, 'It's okay. Someday it will be better.'"

Until conditions do get better, the U.S. has adopted a long-term approach to the park idea, according to Bob Gerhard, who works with the National Park Service's Shared Beringian Heritage Program. "This began as a scientific program focused on natural history and archaeology," he says, "but it has become more of a people-to-people program. We are concerned with ways to bring the people of the two sides together to exchange ideas and information."

Whaling captains from Barrow now travel to Siberia across the Chukchi Sea to teach hunters the age-old skill of taking whales. Elders from Russia rekindle the lost art of Eskimo song and dance among young people in Shishmaref on the Seward Peninsula, while U.S. kids from Savoonga teach the Yupik language to kids from Siberia's Novoye Chaplino. Russian archaeology studies now appear in English. A list of plant and animal names is written in Russian, English, Inupiat, and Siberian Yupik. These are all ribbons of goodwill between places once connected by a land bridge and still connected by blood. Although bigger measures may have to wait, there can be great value in small things, too. As L. Saunders McNeill will tell you, some may be as small as human faces.

Tlingit Charles Jimmie, Sr., a drummer with the Chilkat Dancers, performs at old Fort Seward, near Haines. Now known for its cultural offerings, the port of Haines once served as a gold rush supply center.

This moment in the swirling, time-tangling mists could also be July 17, 1897, when a headline in the *Seattle Post-Intelligencer* changed Alaska forever: "Gold! Gold! Gold! Gold!" The steamship *Portland* had arrived from Alaska carrying 68 prospectors, more than a ton of gold, and enough rags-to-riches stories to spark a stampede. News of one of the richest gold strikes in U.S. history rang out "like a shot from a starter's pistol," as one writer put it. Clerks jumped their counters, trolley drivers quit on the tracks, and Seattle's mayor wired in his resignation; all joined in a race to the Klondike, then part of Canada's Northwest Territories. For many, the first stop was Skagway, Alaska Territory.

"And we're off like a herd of turtles," says Steve Hites, coaxing into motion his 1937 Kenworth, a National Park touring limousine affectionately known as Big Red. To get an overview of Skagway's role in the gold rush, I've signed up for a tour with the Skagway Street Car Company owned by Hites, who is part guide, part historian, and part street actor. "Skagway is theater without walls," he says as spotlights of sun flare on the mountainsides.

Center stage is Broadway, Skagway's main street and the showcase of Klondike Gold Rush National Historical Park. A 12-million-dollar face-lift has restored the street to its glory days: Wooden boardwalks, false-fronted buildings, and horse-drawn carriages give visitors a glimpse of the Skagway that greeted gold seekers when they stepped off the docks in 1897.

And step off the docks they did, by the thousands. The goldfields lay 350 miles north. Still, Skagway became the "Gateway to the Klondike" because of its deepwater port and its proximity to two notches in the Coast Mountains on the British Columbia border. In months, a virtually empty valley was transformed into what was for a time Alaska's largest town. One of the wildest, woolliest places on the continent, Skagway sported 80 saloons and a row of brothels that "satisfied more than a prospector's thirst" with women like Popcorn Kate, who wore "only enough clothes to fill a thimble." There were fistfights and drawn pistols, shell games, scams, even murder. With every sunrise, it seemed, another corpse turned up in the streets, pockets turned inside out.

"The town was called 'little better than hell on Earth,'" Steve Hites says as he backs Big Red up to the cemetery for another one of his stories. "And the devil himself was Jefferson Randolph 'Soapy' Smith—crime boss of Skagway." All that would end with a bang, or rather two bangs, on a July night in 1898.

With rocks for a stage, Hites spins the tale, telling us that on the evening of July 8 the Committee of 101, a vigilante force, was meeting on the wharf to discuss ways to rid the town of its criminal element. "Soapy, plied with whiskey," Hites says in almost a whisper, "grabbed his rifle and headed for the wharf." Frank Reid, the town's surveyor, blocked his way. "'Damn you, Frank, out of my way!' Two shots rang out. *Bang! Bang!*" Hites slaps his hands together to imitate gunfire, then pauses dramatically.

"They buried Soapy over here," he says while gesturing toward an old wooden headboard, "and Frank Reid here," pointing to a granite monument etched with the words "He gave his life for the honor of Skagway." Hites taps the headstone respectfully: "Good shootin', Frank."

Much of Skagway's wildness died with Soapy. You can still hear ragtime piano at the Red Onion Saloon, where closing time is "whenever," but gift shops have replaced bordellos. "The most heinous crime in Skagway these days," Hites says, "is dog-at-large." Today the wildness begins nine miles away at Dyea, Skagway's abandoned former rival at the head of the Chilkoot Trail.

Except for the White Pass route from Skagway, the only overland stretch of the 1,300 miles from Seattle to the Klondike was the Chilkoot Trail, "the meanest 33 miles in history." For 33 muddy, rock-strewn miles between Dyea and Bennett Lake—the western arm of Tagish Lake, which is the source of the upper Yukon River—there was no choice but to walk.

From July 1897 through 1898, 30,000 people did just that, in a "moving circus" of humanity. Then, with the opening of the railroad over White Pass in 1899, the trail fell silent, rarely used and virtually forgotten for more than half a century. Reopened for recreational use in the mid-1960s, the Chilkoot Trail was made part of the Klondike Gold Rush International Historical Park in 1976. Now a hundred people a day strike out during the summer, making up yet another stampede.

Following pages: **Today the Chilkoot Trail, in the distance, attracts thousands of hikers and skiers each year. In 1899 gold seekers abandoned it when the White Pass & Yukon Route opened for business.**

This morning, though, the trailhead at Dyea is deserted. Instantly I am swallowed by rain forest, where water drips from leaves, moss grows in thick tufts, and bell-like sounds come from the Taiya River. I am reminded of the history behind the history. One of the few glacier-free routes from the coast between Juneau and Yakutat to the interior of the state, the Chilkoot was a Tlingit trading route for many years before the stampede. Along this trail the Tlingit carried blankets, cedar boxes, and euchalon (a fish so infused with oil that a wick threaded through its dried body could be lit like the wick of a candle). The footsteps here go much deeper than gold.

But gold rush history dominates the Chilkoot Trail today. Visitors walk in the footsteps of stampeders and feel the same throbbing in their legs, the same tug at the neck from the pack straps, and the same cold rain.

I duck into the warming cabin at the Canyon City campsite, a dusty, mouse-filled spot with the stump of a log chainsawed into a chair. I sit, drying out and reading a stampeder's journal: "We were soon dry, had lots of dry wood, lots of good cooking, and we felt like millionaires." Meanwhile, my cookstove hisses with hot soup.

Two days later, the rain is still falling and my cookstove is still hissing, this time with morning coffee at Sheep Camp, the final stop below timberline. During the stampede 1,500 people a day camped here; as many as 8,000 did when the weather halted their progress. On this site were 16 hotels, 14 restaurants, 3 saloons, and a post office. A hard, haphazard kind of place, the old camp was "the vilest hole I have ever seen," said one stampeder, "not so by nature but made so by man." Today the camp (*Continued on page 150*)

From the 1848 gold discovery on the Kenai Peninsula to the hundreds of claims still worked today, gold (above) has lined the dreams, and the pockets, of many Alaskans. The largest nugget yet found in the state weighed 294 troy ounces and has a current worth of more than $100,000. Perhaps even more riches await discovery in the Chatanika River (right), just off the Steese Highway northeast of Fairbanks.

Following pages: With a touch of gold and an abundance of green, the northern lights—aurora borealis—flicker in the night sky over the Yukon River. Such displays fill the heavens as solar particles enter Earth's upper atmosphere and interact with the magnetic field.

In the wake of the 19th-century gold seekers, a group of German adventurers set out down the Yukon River in their homemade raft. "Just like in the gold rush days, people still come from all over the world to float the Yukon," says ranger Kevin Fox of Yukon-Charley Rivers National Preserve.

"The miners wanted to name this town 'Ptarmigan,' but none of them could spell it," says Susan Wiren. She has seen many a miner come and go through the swinging doors of the only saloon in Chicken, Alaska, about 30 miles west of the Canadian border.

(Continued from page 141) is peaceful: A small creek flows clear as fresh air; there are a few rotting logs, scraps of iron, and in one spot an old shoe.

From Sheep Camp the Chilkoot Trail is a stairway to the clouds, gaining 2,800 vertical feet in just over three and a half miles. It leads directly through an avalanche path, where trees that had been snapped like matchsticks now serve as reminders of the darkest moment in Chilkoot history—April 3, 1898, Palm Sunday. "The mountains will move today," a local packer had warned, but few people heeded his words. Before day's end, an avalanche roared off the mountains above Sheep Camp and killed about 60 stampeders, many of them now buried in the Slide Cemetery near the trailhead. I walk quickly and silently past the spot.

Following a lone set of footprints, I come to The Scales, a rocky, flat perch at the foot of the Chilkoot's steepest pitch. This had been the moment of truth for the stampeders. Ahead of them lay a gut-wrenching climb of 800 feet in a half mile, including 1,378 steps carved in ice that became known as "the Golden Stairs." To prevent mass starvation among the would-be miners, Canada's North West Mounted Police had required each person coming over the pass to bring at least 1,150 pounds of supplies—enough food and gear to last through one winter. People would carry as much as they could in one trip up the Golden Stairs and then go back for another load. Step after step. Gray rock after gray rock. Again and again. Dreams might have gotten the gold seekers this far, but sinew and sweat got them up from here.

The air around The Scales in the winter of 1898-99 rang with what one witness called a "single, all encompassing groan," the voice of misery as thousands of men, women, and children, single file, struggled over the pass. In their eyes they carried visions of wealth. In their hearts they carried the dreams of a nation mired in economic hard times. On their backs they carried picks and shovels, supplies for the winter. Sometimes, a few surprising things were brought along as well.

"A piano," I say and repeat the words like a mantra as I pull myself up the next boulder. Reciting a list of things stampeders once hauled over these mountains will, I hope, make my backpack seem lighter. I take another step, slowly, waiting to be certain of my balance before shifting my weight forward into the 45-degree slope. "A flock of live chickens." The wind rips at my hood, making it flap like a startled bird. "A plow," I say aloud, recalling one Iowa farm boy who hefted a 125-pound plow up the pass on a bet. "Rocking chairs and whiskey." Finally, out of the fog looms the summit cabin and a hiker from Manitoba, whose footprints I have been following. We celebrate the climb with hot chocolate and dry socks while the wind rattles the cabin windows.

After the stampeders had made the difficult journey over the pass, they still faced miles of rocky terrain as well as 500 lake and river miles to get to Dawson and the goldfields. Yet, with Chilkoot Pass behind them, the way seemed to slide easily into a "new and smiling country," where bluebells bloomed like notes of music and the sun shimmered off water flowing toward gold. But first they had to build boats, then wait for the ice to go out at Bennett Lake. On May 29, 1898, with a hiss and a boom, it did go out, followed over the next few days by about 7,000 boats. The stampeders, many of whom were shouting and singing with joy, were on their way again. That joy wouldn't last.

Though 500 million dollars in gold would be mined from the Klondike goldfields, most of the stampeders in Dawson got there too late to share in the wealth. Virtually every inch of Bonanza and Eldorado Creeks, which had set off the rush, had been staked and claimed before most of the stampeders had even left their homes. Of the 100,000 people who started out for the Klondike, only a few thousand of them ever actually panned for gold. Fewer still got rich.

Some turned for home. Others, like E. A. "Nimrod" Robertson, drifted farther down the Yukon River, looking to start a new life. A "cultured Scottish gentleman from Maine," Robertson came over the Chilkoot Trail in 1898 dreaming of making $1,000 to fund his ideas for

"Give me enough snoose and dynamite and I'll build you a road to hell," boasted engineer Michael Heney. In 26 months he built the White Pass & Yukon Route out of Skagway, a feat many thought impossible.

building a flying machine. When things didn't pan out for him, he built and operated a jewelry store in Eagle. He also set up camp on Flume Creek off the Seventymile River, a tributary of the Yukon, to trap animals and cut wood.

Inventive and resourceful, Robertson fashioned a set of homemade dentures—bear teeth for molars, Dall sheep and caribou teeth in front—when he lost his own teeth to scurvy; he wore those dentures happily for 25 years. He is also remembered for creating an accurate relief map of the Yukon from moose blood and newspaper, a map that was displayed at the 1962 World's Fair in Seattle, Washington.

In 1940, by then in his eighties, Nimrod Robertson was caught by a fall storm while prospecting along the Seventymile. He decided to head home by way of a little-used shortcut over a mountain, but halfway back he realized he was too weak to continue. Afraid of being eaten by wild animals, he set his rifle against a tree and lay back in a small creek, hoping with his last act to keep the animals away from his body. "He died as he loved to live," one memorial said of him, "alone in the woods." That and frozen in a block of ice.

"This country is full of stories like Nimrod Robertson's," says Kevin Fox, chief of operations at Yukon-Charley Rivers National Preserve, as we motor past the mouth of the Seventymile River on the broad back of the Yukon. Just a few miles into Alaska, the Yukon River flows light brown and shot through with silver. A fringe of soft green willow lines the gravel bars while a stubble of black spruce sprouts from the mountains that seem to roll off endlessly on both banks. Created in 1980, the 2.5-million-acre Yukon-Charley Rivers National Preserve commemorates the gold rush and protects the wildlands in those seemingly endless mountains.

"When you come across a big ol' relic like this," Fox says later as we climb atop a rusting steam tractor slowly sinking into a bog, "it really hits you how much greener it is around here than it was during the heyday of the gold rush." Whole towns with names such as Star City, Nation, and Ivy have vanished. Forests once sheared to feed the ravenous appetites of steamboats are growing back. Gold rush or no gold rush, the wilderness still dominates.

Just ask Paul Trussell and Greg Seats. We come across the two hikers, red-eyed from campfire smoke and wild-haired, far up a tributary of the Yukon. For them, this is day 23 of a planned 85-day hike. "We did a 45-day trip in Gates of the Arctic," Greg tells us while rolling his own cigarette beside a smudge fire lit to keep the bugs at bay. "Then we said, 'Let's double it next year,' and the plan was hatched."

With a third hiker they refer to only as "Joe," who is nowhere to be seen, they had planned to float the Yukon to the Nation, hike the mountains into Canada, and take another river back to the Yukon. In all, the journey would comprise 300 miles of trail-less, make-you-weak-in-the-knees wilderness.

After 18 days of rain, bugs, and 120-pound packs in a maze of swamp and downed timber, Joe called it quits, opting to stay behind and "meditate" for a couple of months until the others got back. "It might have had something to do with the bear-spray incident," Paul says, smiling. Joe had gotten spooked and taken the safety cap off his bear-repellent spray. When he bent down to wash a pot, the repellent escaped, dousing him with hot pepper mace. He threw the pot into the river and then dived in after it, howling in pain.

Despite storms and nearly getting swept away while crossing a river, Paul and Greg say they are determined to continue, drawn by the lure of a long wilderness journey. "After about 30 days in the bush it stops being a trip and becomes more of a lifestyle," Paul says. "You settle into the pace of things."

"Besides," Greg tells us as he rolls another cigarette, "we are just starting to figure out how skinny we'll get!"

We take a packet of postcards to mail for them and wave good-bye to Paul and Greg. "I had thought about trying to talk them out of it when they first called about maps," Kevin says. "But this is one of the last places where you can really be on your own if you want to be. In the end, this is wilderness and it's their call."

Five days after that meeting, rangers picked Joe up when a fisherman reported encountering someone trying to flag down a boat on the Yukon. Paul and Greg, however, continued their journey for two months, getting drenched by rains, baked by heat, and stranded in the river by a forest fire. On day 69 they showed up back in town tired and hungry, but happy and safe.

"On the way out," Paul told me later, "we met a trapper who said, 'Boys, you are headed into some of the wildest country left on the planet. I doubt you can make it, but if you do, then you can call yourselves tough guys.'" The two didn't finish the route they had planned, but when they ran into the man again in Eagle, they reintroduced themselves. "Hello," they said to him. "We are two 'tough guys.'"

During my last night on the Yukon River—far from those rising mists at Serpentine Hot Springs—I walk downstream from camp and think about time. A pair of swans flies low along the water, their feathers rose-red in the late light. Inches from my boots one of the largest, most storied rivers on this continent flows by at six miles an hour. Tons of water pass by each second, yet the river moves so silently that the low hum of a bee worrying the wildflowers can be heard a dozen yards away.

Earlier in the day Kevin Fox had pulled our boat up onto a gravel bar to show me something on the bank: a complex collection of wires and solar panels hidden in the brush. "It is a satellite water-gauging station," he said. "You can log on to your computer and from the comfort of your own home check the level of the river in real-time readouts."

"Real time." The words sound strange as I walk next to a river that flowed just like this thousands of years before Blue Babe was killed by lions. Once an ice-free corridor for nomadic hunters who crossed the Bering land bridge, the Yukon has carried steamboats and stampeders, solitude seekers and wilderness dreamers. It flows like time—patient and unceasing, the decades and the centuries worn as smooth as river stones by its passing.

"Real time," I think to myself, tossing a branch into the current. With the midnight sun warm on my face, I watch the branch bob off downstream until it is lost in a mist now rising off the water, and then I start back for camp. Behind me, the Yukon River is still flowing beside a string of my footprints in the sand, footprints that will be gone with the next wave, the next wind, the next passing of time. ▲

Not everyone will discover gold, but anyone can find a
wealth of natural resources in Alaska, where the bounty
of the land still provides food for many residents.
For Jim Gelvin (above) of Central, just off the Steese
Highway, a bull moose means meat for the winter.
North of Anchorage, Don Dinkel and Dawg (opposite)
visit Dinkel's field near Wasilla to show off an immense
cabbage grown beneath the midnight sun.

Following pages: Fingers of fog reach into narrow valleys and cling to hillsides, obscuring time and rivers but also creating unforgettable vistas along the Top of the World Highway east of Jack Wade, Alaska.

Pages 158-59: Dreams of gold—perhaps even pots of it at the ends of a perfect rainbow—have drawn adventurers to the wild horizons of the Yukon River for decades. Perhaps they always will.

CHAPTER 5

Wild at Heart

Sometime during the night the snow stopped falling, the sky cleared, and a wolverine crossed the field behind the cabin north of Fairbanks. I know all this from tracks I follow to the creek, where I will chop ice to melt for water; those tracks are a curious comfort, a kind of company after days of being alone. Since I arrived a week ago, a storm has sat down hard on this valley, drifting snow nearly to the cabin windows. I have grown so accustomed to the low howling of the wind—like wolves far off—that at night I wake when it stops, aware of a great silence. All around me the landscape has emptied: The bears have holed up in their dens; the salmon have spawned and died; and the birds of summer have spilled over the southern horizon, leaving the sky a bare alabaster shell. In winter, Alaska can be a lonely place.

After such a season, the explosion of life that follows can appear nothing short of a miracle—like the time Chatham Strait seemed to fill up with whales. On that summer day in 1984, Cynthia D'Vincent of the Intersea Foundation of Carmel Valley, California, had spent hours photographing humpbacks and recording their songs from a small skiff. The whales were swimming, feeding, and singing nearby, but then they came much closer. "I had packed up my gear, and my hydrophone was out of the water, yet I could still hear the songs through the hull of the boat and even in the air," she recalls. "They have to be pretty close for that to happen." Next she noticed that herring had quit jumping: "It was eerie, like when birds stop singing just before a storm."

One by one, large bubbles burst at the surface, slowly encircling the boat. Peering down, D'Vincent saw "the white flash of pectoral fins—a lot of pectoral fins," as whales rushed after the herring. Suddenly, nine humpbacks broke the surface of the "bubble net" in unison, the final flourish of a complex behavior known as cooperative feeding. Herring began leaping into the boat, wiggling masses of frightened fish flopping against D'Vincent's rubber boots. Whales surrounded her: "Everywhere I looked there were these great jaws rising over me as the lower jaws slid under the boat."

Then they were gone. "The whales were so intent on feeding that they were not aware of me until the last second," she says. "When they finally did see me they veered off, never touching me or the boat; they came up a little way off, feeding as if nothing had happened."

Among 15 whale species that swim in Alaskan waters, humpbacks fast all winter in the warm ocean off Hawaii and Mexico, then move north in summer to gorge themselves off the coast of Alaska. With immense jaws gaping, they swim through clouds of swirling sea life, scooping up 500 gallons of water in one gulp. They seine their catch through curtains of baleen, gathering 100-pound mouthfuls of shrimp, herring, and krill that add up to about 4,000 pounds of food a day. Once threatened with extinction, humpbacks now number about 37,000 worldwide, though that is still just 10 to 15 percent of pre-hunting figures.

Previous pages: **All legs and ears and energy, a moose calf high-steps up the Brooks River in Katmai National Park and Preserve. A bull moose can reach 1,800 pounds on a diet of aquatic plants and willow, birch, and aspen twigs.**

"Humpbacks are the most sophisticated feeders among the baleen whales, with complex songs an integral part of their feeding strategy," says D'Vincent. While their summer feeding songs last only about a minute, the winter courting songs can last half an hour or, in sequence, go on for hours. "On the breeding grounds they all sing the same song, but on the feeding grounds each group sings a different song. It may be their signature, the song that identifies their group," she says. "You cannot be out there listening in a small boat without it affecting you. Sometimes after work, when everyone else on the ship would go to bed, I would go out in my boat, put my hydrophone in the water, and just listen." The sounds are deep and unearthly, as if the ocean itself were singing.

At times the sky also seems to be singing, the air filling with the songs and calls of birds that annually pour into the state. Every summer a hundred million birds nest in the Yukon and Kuskokwim Deltas, and each winter 3,000 bald eagles decorate trees along the Chilkat River. The sky of the state's interior is sliced with the feathered lightning strikes of peregrines and tufted with flocks of redpolls, spiraling like sparks from a campfire.

And then there are the western sandpipers, which stop for a while at the Copper River Delta on their way to western Alaska. "Several million birds pass through our delta every spring," says Kelley Weaverling, president of the local Audubon chapter and a former mayor of Cordova.

"We have good numbers out here today," adds Mary Anne Bishop of the Prince William Sound Science Center. "Not tens of thousands, but good numbers." Weaverling, Bishop, and I are walking the edge of Hartney Bay south of Cordova, our rubber boots slurping in the mud; the bay is the focal point of the Copper River Delta Shorebird Festival. Out on the mudflats, the falling tide has left a silver sheen that reflects the sky and doubles the peaks as if the world is staring at itself in a mirror. Dotting that mirror are thousands of western sandpipers.

On the ground a western sandpiper is not very impressive. Six inches long, weighing only an ounce, and speckled brown in spring, with a quiver of arrowhead-shaped streaks along its breast, a single bird is just a speck against the vast delta. But in the air, flocks dance; there is no other word for it. They dance with air and light and waves, all the birds in perfect step, twirling in unison, flashing the white undersides of thousands of pairs of wings. Then come the dainty splashes, like tinkling bells, as they land again to feed.

It is impossible to stand on the mudflats at twilight, basking in the last flecks of light left in a May evening, and not be glad that the world has such beauty in it, glad for the existence of these small birds, dancing and feeding.

"They eat almost constantly while here," says Bishop. "Day and night they are feeding on small invertebrates, mostly tiny *Macoma* clams and fly larvae, because they need a lot of food to replenish their energy. One bird is known to have traveled 1,900 miles from San Francisco Bay to the Copper River in less than two days."

Watching sandpipers on the flats, their thin bills darning the mud like sewing needles, I think they seem too frail to have crossed continents. Yet each spring these small birds, hardly bigger than mouthfuls of air, leave wintering grounds as far south as Peru and begin slowly hopscotching along the Pacific coast, traveling 100 to 300 miles before stopping to rest. They work their way north, setting down to rest and feed at the same wetlands shorebirds have used for thousands of years: San Francisco Bay; Grays Harbor in Washington; the Fraser River Delta in British Columbia; and the Stikine River Delta, small estuaries around Yakutat, and Copper River Delta in Alaska.

Soon the sandpipers will move again, to nesting grounds at the mouth of the Yukon. "I like to think of this place as a Howard   *(Continued on page 174)*

Testing the winds, a horned puffin (opposite) on Round Island gets set for takeoff. Puffins "fly" underwater nearly as well as they do in the air, chasing the fish that make up most of their diet.

Following pages: Blurred wings stir the air at Hartney Bay, where as many as four million migrating western sandpipers stop to feed and rest.

Pages 168-69: From the waters of Turnagain Arm, coho salmon must run a gantlet of fishermen waiting on the banks of Bird Creek.

164

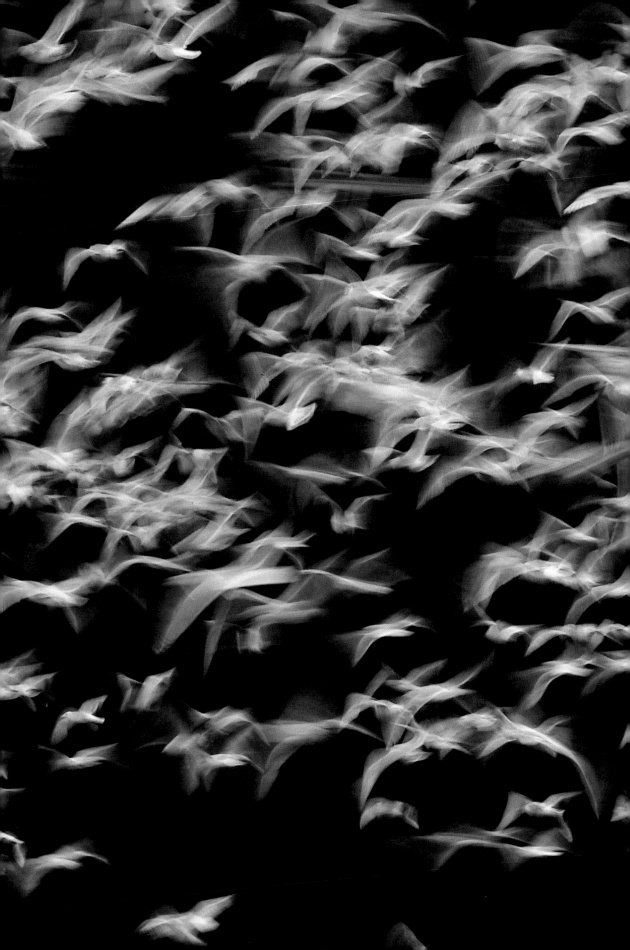

Highly social birds, thick-billed murres lay their eggs on bare cliffs crowded with other murres. To feed themselves and their young, they dive as deep as 390 feet to snag herring and other small fish in the waters surrounding the Pribilof Islands.

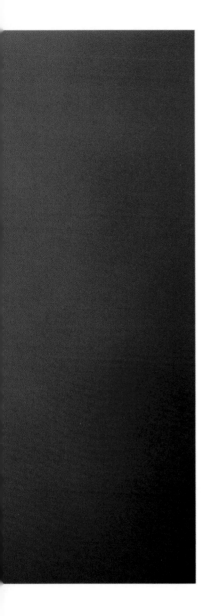

In swirls of black feathers and orange beaks, crested auklets sometimes form immense flocks that dive and spiral as if painting the sky. Members of this bird species have a unique feature: They smell like citrus.

Following pages: A trumpeter swan fluffs its feathers beside Alaganik Slough in the Copper River Delta. Each spring, 5 percent of the world's 16,000 trumpeter swans come to the delta to nest.

(*Continued from page 164*) Johnson's on their route," Weaverling says. "They travel so far, and then they have to stop and recharge their batteries."

"The Copper River Delta supports the highest concentration of migratory shorebirds in the Western Hemisphere," says Bishop. At 700,000 acres, it is the largest contiguous wetland on the Pacific coast. As many as four million western sandpipers—80 percent of the world's population—and most of the Pacific population of dunlins use the delta. It is the nesting ground for 5 percent of the world's 16,000 trumpeter swans and the only known nesting spot for the dusky Canada goose. Ducks come from Baja California; songbirds and shorebirds fly from Central and South America as well as from Africa. If birds left tracks in the sky, the world's nations would be tied together with ribbons of flight, ribbons that can be very fragile: The Wilderness Society recently listed the Copper River Delta as one of the 15 most endangered wild places in the United States. A road proposed by the Chugach Alaska Corporation (CAC) would cut into the delta, providing access to 77,000 acres of timberland and coal deposits east of the river; it would also threaten water quality, disturb salmon-spawning beds, and endanger marshes used by birds.

With a sharp eye for the Eyak River's shifting sandbars, guide Andy Craig of Cordova maneuvers his boat through the Copper River Delta, largest intact wetland on the Pacific coast of North America.

"The CAC believes the land is worthless if they don't extract resources," says Dune Lankard, an opponent of the proposed road. He is a member of the Eyak nation—the smallest group of Alaska natives—and founder of the Eyak Rainforest Preservation Fund. "From the Eyak perspective, the land could never be considered worthless. It provides subsistence, spirituality, and sovereignty." For millions of birds, this land also provides an irreplaceable link in a cycle of migration as ancient as the sky, a respite in a world stitched together with wings.

Birds aren't the only things with wings that stir the Alaskan sky; other creatures do, too, including some that people may not expect. "I've had people look me straight in the eye and say there are no butterflies in Alaska," laughs Kenelm Philip, one of the world's leading experts on Arctic butterflies. "And on more than one occasion," he says as he tugs on rubber boots,

"I've had the distinct pleasure of being able to reply, 'Of course there are and, well, there goes one now.'" In fact, the state is home to 83 confirmed butterfly species, including mourning cloak and green comma, silvery blue and hoary elfin, red admiral, painted lady, and titania fritillary. Many were first documented by Philip, whom I join for a hike in the Bonanza Creek Experimental Forest outside Fairbanks. On a perfect June afternoon with puffy white clouds and a soft breeze, we will see if any of those 83 species are on the wing.

"People think Alaskan winters are too much for butterflies, but actually summer is the limiting factor," Philip explains, his eyes scanning the bushes. "Aha!" he shouts, swinging the net so near my head that I instinctively duck. "That looks like *Limenitis arthemis.*" A white admiral. "Sorry. I grew up using the scientific names," he says, carefully untangling and releasing the butterfly. "Butterflies survive the winter just fine. Some winter over as larvae; others, like *Polygonia faunus*, hibernate under the snow, their bodies so full of glycerol that people say they taste sweet, though I've never tested that for myself." What butterflies really need are enough dry, warm summer days for feeding, mating, and laying eggs. The Aleutian Islands with mild winters but cool summers have almost no butterflies, while the Brooks Range, with brutal winters but warm and dry summers, has many. More than half of Alaska's butterfly species are found on the North Slope.

"The tundra is my favorite place in the world," says Philip, who has collected all over Alaska, the Yukon, even in Arctic Russia. "I find the idea that butterflies can flourish in such a harsh environment completely fascinating." To do that, they have had to adapt: Species on the Arctic coasts of Alaska and Canada tend to be darker to soak up the sun's heat. They press their wings against sun-warmed rocks or use them like reflectors to direct heat to their bodies. Some crawl more than they fly, avoiding strong winds. In a cool, wet summer, some remain in hibernation, postponing the completion of their life cycle until the following year.

"Oh, oh, that's one I want," Philip says, spotting dark wings against the sky. At 68 he is a stout man, round in the middle. But when he spots a butterfly, he becomes a hunter, stalking in a low crouch and often saying the Latin name when he moves in, as if the name itself will lure the butterfly into his net; then, *whish*, he snatches the creature from the air. He turns it over, pinches the thorax to immobilize it, and drops it into a glassine envelope.

With nearly 100,000 specimens, Philip's personal collection of North American Arctic butterflies is second only to the Canadian National Collection and will eventually be housed in the Smithsonian. "At first, of course, you do it because they are beautiful," he says, "but as you get to know any group of creatures, you become attracted to the unsolved problems. With Alaska's butterflies there are unsolved problems in taxonomy, life history, and even simple things, such as where they came from and what the population trends might be." Catching a flutter of wings over my shoulder, he suddenly shouts "Hello there!" And with that, Kenelm Philip is stalking across the tussocks, about to add another piece to the complex and beautiful puzzle of Alaska's butterflies.

"That would make a great jigsaw puzzle," says Mary Cody, a biologist with the U.S. Fish and Wildlife Service. From the cliffs of Round Island, in the Walrus Islands State Game Sanctuary, she is watching a mass of bull walruses flopped all akimbo on the rocks below. Hundreds are stacked together flipper to flipper and tusk to tail "like hogges upon heapes," in the words of a 17th-century sailor. "Puppy piles," Cody calls them. Some lie on their bulbous bellies. Others flop on their backs, flippers spread wide, heads lolling in formal, operatic poses as if they may at any moment break into song. Instead, they grunt—deep-throated, gut-rumbling, nasal-flapping grunts.

This three-mile-long island in Bristol Bay is the longest continuously used *ugli*, or walrus haul-out, in North America. Even in the mid-1800s, when depleted whale stocks led to overhunting of walruses and the abandonment of many other haul-outs, walruses still came to Round Island. In 1982 walruses also began showing up at Cape Peirce in Togiak National Wildlife Refuge, the first mainland Alaska haul-out since the 1870s. Their numbers were climbing again, thanks in part to the Marine Mammal Protection Act. Alaskan waters are now home to about 200,000 Pacific walruses, which are hunted only by native groups. In villages like Gambell and Savoonga, on St. Lawrence Island, the hides are used for skin boats, the blubber for oil, and the stomach membranes for drum skins. "We rely on the walrus," Carl Kava, director of the Eskimo Walrus Commission in Nome, has said. "It is a big part of our diet and our tradition. Without it, I think we would be somewhat lost."

Every summer, while female walruses are off on ice floes with their young, thousands of males return to Round Island, where they rest after feeding in surrounding waters. Each day walruses eat about a hundred pounds apiece, diving as deep as 300 feet and staying under for 30 minutes. They siphon up clams, snails, and other mollusks, then use their powerful tongues to remove the meat. Bellies full, they swim back to the haul-out, laboriously pulling themselves up rocky beaches and groaning like fat old men. They jostle and jab, poking with their long tusks, bellowing with indignation. Finally, they plop down with immense nasal sighs.

"They're so funny," Cody says, watching a big bull, white with cold, trying to force its two-ton body in among a mound of smaller, already sleeping bulls. "They work very hard to get close and then complain about it."

Three times a day Cody and her co-workers traverse the island to count walruses—a species whose life history, surprisingly, is still not well known. Much of a walrus's time is spent out of sight on the ice or underwater, and many haul-outs are on the Russian side of the Bering Strait, where there is little money for research. Even population figures are only estimates: The last reliable census was completed in 1990.

"I wish we knew what was going on with them," Cody says in a quiet moment. "They are just so different from other animals I've studied. With some animals you get a sense of what they are up to, but with walruses we really don't have a clue."

One mystery lies in the complex array of sounds walruses make. Besides the usual grunts and groans filling a windless day at Round Island, there are knocks, whistles, and an almost ethereal call known as chiming—"among the most strangely beautiful sounds in the world," says Kathy Turco, a nature-sound recording artist who often comes to the island. She started out as a scientist studying walrus thermoregulation but became intrigued with chiming; she now travels the state recording natural sounds. "Birdcalls, whale songs, the chiming of walruses—animals communicate in many ways, and we can't hope to truly know a species unless we at least try to understand the sounds they make."

Following pages: In Bristol Bay's Walrus Islands State Game Sanctuary, hundreds of male Pacific walruses crowd the shores of Round Island, relaxing after feeding in surrounding waters.

Chiming seems to be done most often in the water, with walruses inflating their pharyngeal pouches and somehow moving that air around. "Bulls practice making the sound in summer, floating just offshore," Turco says. "Then, during the breeding season, they dance underwater, singing a chorus of clicks, knocks, gongs, and chimes to attract females." Chiming's soft, musical tone—"their love song"—is almost sensual, as if harp strings were being strummed by wind. "I was sitting in the tall grass one summer day," recalls Turco. "The air was vibrating with chimes. It was so beautiful and peaceful that I fell asleep and dreamed of naked men parading by on ice floes!"

I don't dream of naked men on ice floes; I imagine mythical Sirens luring sailors to the shore with their singing. Two tons of wrinkled skin and three-foot tusks may seem an unlikely source for such a sweet sound, but then nature can be like that. All night, as I lie dozing in my tent, a lone walrus floats in the bay, chiming the hours, filling the air with music.

This is a memory, not my imagination: Our canoes round a bend in the Kobuk River and scrape to a stop on a small spit of beach. In the thick air of a three-day rain we stand around fresh tracks in the sand, staring at sharp lines, unbroken edges, claw marks crisp even in the rain. Grizzly. No other creature in North America could have made those tracks.

Grizzlies prowl the mind of anyone in bear country, and Alaska is bear country. Nowhere else in the U.S. do all three North American bear species— black, polar, and brown or grizzly—occur within (Continued on page 186)

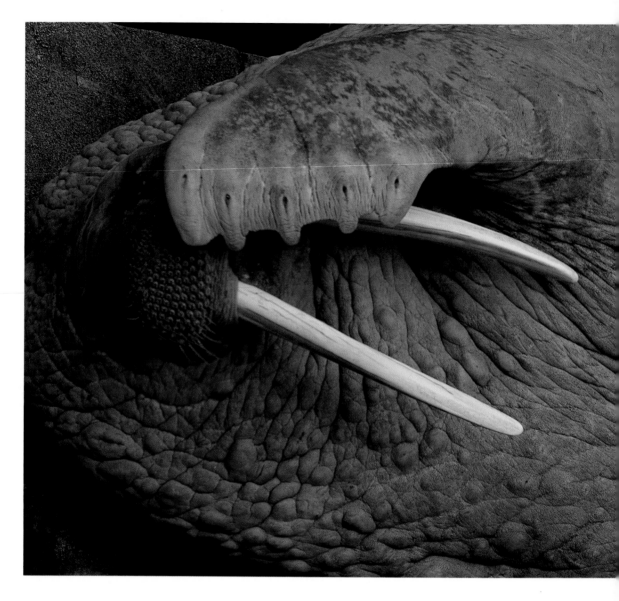

Nearly white when it emerges from the cold water, a walrus gradually reddens as blood returns to its two-inch-thick hide. This large male uses a flipper for an eyeshade while warming itself in the sun.

Opposite: A walrus skull rests among wildflowers on Round Island, an important haul-out site for countless generations of walruses.

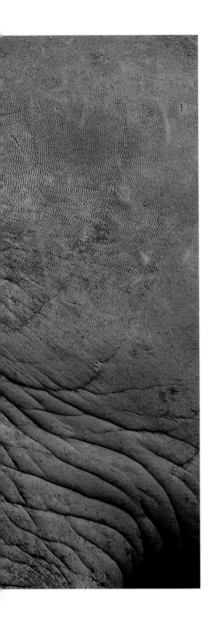

Following pages: Prized for their thick, waterproof pelts, fur seals like these in the Pribilofs once drew Russian merchants to Alaska. The Alaska Maritime National Wildlife Refuge now protects many haul-out sites.

Pages 184-85: In an annual rite of passage, enormous numbers of returning sockeye salmon streak Alaskan rivers red each fall. Biologists along the Kvichak River, part of the Bristol Bay fishery, have documented more than a million salmon migrating upstream in one day.

(*Continued from page 177*) the boundaries of a single state. Wherever you stand, you are never far from bears—and neither are your thoughts. That is particularly true at Brooks Camp in Katmai National Park and Preserve.

"Step off the plane quickly and stay together," ranger Katherine Johnson says as the propeller of the Twin Otter chugs to a stop at the edge of Naknek Lake. "A female is coming this way just down the beach." We have not yet stepped off the floatplane, and already we are seeing our first bear.

Each summer hundreds of thousands of salmon course up the Brooks River as it flows from Brooks Lake. This frenzy of fish attracts brown bears, which come here to gorge themselves on sockeye salmon. The spectacle of up

Milking the bounty, a biologist with the Prince William Sound Aquaculture Corporation will use this male sockeye salmon to help fertilize some of the 35 million eggs in the company's hatchery at Paxson.

to 50 large bears along a mile and a half of riverbank also attracts as many as 200 humans a day, creating perhaps the greatest concentration of fish, people, and bears anywhere in the world.

"Our job basically is to manage the people more than the bears," Johnson tells me as we walk the trail toward the lower viewing platform after an orientation program. "With any decision we make, our first concern is whether it is good for the bears." She says all visitors to Brooks Camp must attend the orientation session. They must store their food in elevated caches and remember to clap, sing, or make noise on the trails. They should keep at least 100 yards away from bears with young (50 yards for the other bears). Fishermen are told to cut their lines if bears come close, because bears have learned a bent fly rod means a meal is on the hook.

For the most part, this "truce" has worked well: Brooks Camp hasn't had a serious bear-caused injury to a human in nearly 40 years. There is no record of a person having been killed by a bear here, and no bear has had to be destroyed since 1983. Instead, bears are "hazed" with cracker shells and rubber bullets if they display aggressive behavior or are habitually attracted to cabins and campgrounds. They are kept out of food caches by electric fences and can be viewed from a pair of elevated platforms, where a battalion of Park Service personnel keeps bears and humans at a safe distance.

"The bears are the intelligent ones," Johnson says as we watch a pair of fishermen walk unaware past a bear bedded down in the grass less than 20 yards away. "They are not attacking us every time we do stupid things."

"People think we can view the bears this closely because they are tame," she continues. "They are not. These are wild animals. There is just so much food—and so many other bears—that their tolerance is way up. We are like bugs to them, so they don't even notice us. Believe me, when bears have nightmares, people are not causing their bad dreams; other bears are."

Some people might find that hard to believe. As two armed rangers hold back a group of visitors on the trail, a woman in a red scarf is shrieking: "Oh! Oh! Okay. Just tell me where to stand. Right here? Is this safe?"

"We always give bears the right-of-way," says Katherine Johnson.

The bears we've stopped for wander off in a few minutes, and the trail is reopened. People move on, except for the woman in red who has seen enough. She turns back for the safety of the lodge.

For most visitors, the reaction to seeing a bear is much different. "When people come over the rise to the upper platform and for the first time see a bear at the falls, it takes their breath away," says Jane Frobose, a park volunteer. "It is a dream-come-true kind of experience."

At the platform 40 people stand shoulder-to-shoulder, tripod-to-tripod, but no bears are seen. Instead, we watch hundreds of sockeyes leaping from the foamy water and hurling themselves at the falls. The sight makes me recall something Katherine Johnson had said earlier: "The bears are beautiful, but I tell people to take a moment and appreciate the salmon that drive the whole ecosystem. If they weren't here, the bears wouldn't be here either."

The bears, however, are what people come to see. Soon, a big male lumbers into the pool beneath the falls; another, an open wound on its flank, makes its way to the lip of the falls above. Because bears have just six months to eat enough food to build up fat, competition for prime fishing spots can be fierce. Each four-and-a-half-pound sockeye contains about 4,600 fat-rich calories that will help a hungry bear get through the winter.

Year after year many of the same bears—Ester and Goatee, Cinnamon and Beauty, Panda and Gramps—return to the falls, becoming fixtures in the park. Diver, the most famous and most photographed of the Brooks Falls bears, is known for submerging completely and chasing schools of salmon, which scatter like buckshot. On this day, the big bear in the plunge pool simply lowers its muzzle and, with an explosion of spray, clamps a salmon in its jaws, retreating to the bushes to eat. Cameras click and video cameras whirl. On the platform, someone applauds.

For all the thrill of Brooks Camp, there is an air of unreality about viewing bears in a crowded and controlled setting; something is missing. As author Harold McCraken once wrote, seeing a bear in the wild should be "the climax of a thousand dreams and ten years of hoping."

It often happens suddenly. A movement catches your eye: a grizzly crossing the shallows downstream. The sight quickens you. Later, you will find yourself remembering things—the colors of the wildflowers, the slant of light glinting off a wet rock—that otherwise would go unnoticed. You will recall the tilt of the animal's head, the way its nose stabbed the air searching for a scent. You will remember that your heart raced and your fists clenched long after the bear vanished over the ridge. But for the moment, you are alone with the bear, an Alaskan grizzly streaked with autumn's last light as it follows the creek and then turns to strike for the mountains. Even long after it is gone, you are still watching, waiting. Only then do you remember to breathe.

The sound is like a beating heart, or the stomping of hooves. On an August night in 2000, Gwich'in children are dancing inside the candle-lit community hall in Arctic Village. Dressed in tanned caribou shirts and wearing moccasins made from caribou hide, they dance to the beat of drums stretched with caribou skin. "We are caribou people," Gwich'in Sarah James had told me earlier. "The caribou are everything to us."

In Alaska, the caribou outnumber the people: Nearly a million animals make up 32 herds across the state. About 150,000 caribou are in the Mulchatna herd in the vicinity of Lake Clark National Park and Preserve, while as many as 430,000 are in the western Arctic herd in the Brooks Range.

Each spring, the 130,000-animal Porcupine caribou herd starts toward the coastal plain on the Beaufort Sea from wintering grounds in the Yukon Territory and Alaska. Pregnant females go first, bulls and subadults later. The caribou move north and west, swimming frigid streams, crossing mountain passes, and enduring storms. They follow the snow line into the 19.6-million-acre Arctic National Wildlife Refuge and Ivvavik National Park in the Yukon Territory, angling for the coast. When at last they reach the coastal plain, the females give birth—in the same area some people would like to drill for oil.

About 3.2 billion barrels of economically recoverable oil may lie beneath the calving grounds. That's enough, oil companies say, to meet U.S. demand for six months, but it's not enough, conservationists counter, to put at risk the "biological heart" of the Arctic Refuge. "Developing the refuge for oil would be a senseless act equivalent to burning a painting by Van Gogh or Picasso to warm yourself," says Allen Smith, Alaska regional director of the Wilderness Society. "It would destroy this wilderness, ruin habitat for grizzlies, wolves, arctic foxes, golden eagles, millions of migratory birds, the Porcupine caribou herd, and put at risk the traditional way of life of the Gwich'in people."

Some 7,500 Gwich'in live in 15 isolated villages in Alaska and northern Canada, where they hunt, fish, and follow one of the most traditional ways of life in North America. More than half the food in their households comes from the land, and almost all of the families have at least one caribou hunter. They depend on the Porcupine caribou herd.

"The future of the Gwich'in and the future of the caribou are the same," Jonathan Solomon of Fort Yukon has said. To ensure that future, Gwich'in representatives went to Washington, D.C., to educate politicians and the public. They wrote to the United Nations Commission on Human Rights. They also organized the Millennium Trek, which wound through villages on both sides of the border and ended at Arctic Village. From there, some Gwich'in went to a place few had ever visited: the caribou birthing grounds.

"The coastal plain is sacred to my people," Sarah James says. "For more than 20,000 years we have hunted the caribou for food, shelter, and clothing, but people never went to the birthing grounds. We wanted to give the caribou mothers time to have their young. Now we have to go to send a message to the rest of America about how important this is to the Gwich'in." As she speaks, the doors to the community hall are flung open: The elders from the Millennium Trek have returned from the coast. A windblown figure strides to the microphone and the drumming stops.

"We went to the heart of the calving grounds," the hunter says, his face hidden by darkness and the ruff of his beaver fur hat. "It was hard. It was cold and windy. We fasted and prayed for the protection of the land, for the caribou to be strong in this time of trouble. We were visited by grizzly, eagle, hawk, and wolf. Also by caribou. The old ones, the spirits of some who've passed, came around and smiled, going like this (he nods for all to see). There were tears. We paid the price, but it was worth it because this is a good place, a good thing for our people. We did it so that we will be strong together, talk together, think together, and stand together to protect the caribou. The Gwich'in have a right to live as we have always lived. We cannot stand by and let our children's heritage be sold to the oil companies. If we lose the caribou, there will be a great silence." His words are followed by a long silence as the people sit in candlelight, contemplating what he has said. Finally, someone begins to drum—the sound is like a heartbeat—and dancing begins again.

In the depth of winter I follow wolverine tracks in the snow, knowing that even in the deepest cold I will find more signs of life, reminders of summer's frenzy. Beneath the ice a wood frog may be hibernating, protected until spring by a kind of "antifreeze" in its blood. From the woods come faint songs of chickadees: Have faith, every note seems to say; spring will come again.

But not today. After gathering ice at the frozen creek, I circle back toward the cabin, leave my own tracks at the door, and step inside to rekindle the fire. Outside, the wolverine is nearing tree line, making for the pass and a valley where the faint scent of caribou trails lightly on the wind. Quietly, snow is falling. It will gather through the night and all the next day, surrounding me with the silence of winter, covering all the tracks. ▲

Oblivious to the snapping of shutters and the whirring of video cameras, brown bears gather every summer to feast on sockeye salmon at Brooks Falls in Katmai National Park and Preserve.

Opposite: Sharp claws and teeth help a bear catch a sockeye at Brooks Falls. Gorging on salmon—each fish contains nearly 5,000 calories—bears lay on fat before beginning their long winter's sleep.

Following pages: Curious but timid, brown bear cubs wait in the grass while their mother fishes along the Brooks River. Male bears dominate the best fishing spots and may threaten cubs that venture out of hiding.

Pages 194-95: "The grey shepherds of the tundra pass like islands of smoke," writes Alaskan poet John Haines about the caribou that move south each autumn. As they travel, the herds seem to pull winter's white blanket down the mountains behind them.

NOTES ON THE AUTHOR AND PHOTOGRAPHER

Jeff Rennicke, a former wilderness guide in Gates of the Arctic National Park and Preserve, has written more than 250 articles for such publications as *National Geographic Traveler, Backpacker, Reader's Digest,* and *Sierra.* He is the author or co-author of nine books and is a recipient of the Lowell Thomas Travel Journalism Award presented by the Society of American Travel Writers. Jeff lives in Bayfield, Wisconsin, with his wife and two daughters.

Michael Melford's assignments have taken him around the world. His award-winning work appears regularly in *National Geographic Traveler, Fortune, Smithsonian, Coastal Living,* and *Travel Holiday,* as well as in numerous foreign publications. An avid sports enthusiast and general adventurer, he is as comfortable photographing salmon underwater as he is hanging out of a bush plane over Alaska. Michael resides with his family in Mystic, Connecticut.

ACKNOWLEDGMENTS

The Book Division, author, and photographer wish to thank the many individuals, groups, organizations, and federal and state personnel mentioned or quoted in *Treasures of Alaska* for their help and guidance during the book's preparation. We also wish to acknowledge the invaluable assistance of Connie D. Binder, Becky Brock, Joyce M. Caldwell, George Campbell, the Paul and Donna Claus family, Roy Corral and family, Carlann Defontes, Annette Erickson, Faith Gemmill, Trimble Gilbert, Steve Gilroy, Nathan Hamm, Sandy Harbanuk, Bud Hodson, Anne Marie Houppert, Janice Jackson, Jim Lethcoe, Victoria Lord, Eric and Cathy Mofford, Peyton H. Moss, Jr., Kathy Nissley, Tom Quinn, Moses Sam, Leigh Selig, Sue Warner, and Marc Wheeler.

For their support during the writing of this book, the author extends his deepest gratitude to Jill, Katelyn, and Hannah, and to Mike, Kathy, Heather, and Shawn—"the real treasures after all."

ADDITIONAL READING

Readers may wish to consult the *National Geographic Index* for related articles and books. The following titles may also be of interest: Robert Glenn Ketchum, *The Tongass: Alaska's Vanishing Rain Forest* (1987); John McPhee, *Coming into the Country* (1991); Wayne Mergler, ed., *The Last New Land: Stories of Alaska Past and Present* (1996); John Muir, *Travels in Alaska* (1998); Richard K. Nelson, *The Island Within* (1991) and *Make Prayers to the Raven: A Koyukon View of the Northern Forest* (1983); Jeff Rennicke, *Bears of Alaska in Life and Legend* (1987); Robert W. Service, *Collected Poems of Robert Service* (1989); Bill Sherwonit, ed., *Denali: A Literary Anthology* (2000); and Sherry Simpson, *The Way Winter Comes: Alaska Stories* (1998).

INDEX

Treasures of Alaska
LAST GREAT AMERICAN WILDERNESS

By Jeff Rennicke
Photographs by Michael Melford

Published by the National Geographic Society

John M. Fahey, Jr. *President and Chief Executive Officer*

Gilbert M. Grosvenor *Chairman of the Board*

Nina D. Hoffman *Executive Vice President*

Prepared by the Book Division

Kevin Mulroy *Vice President and Editor-in-Chief*

Charles Kogod *Illustrations Director*

Barbara A. Payne *Editorial Director*

Marianne Koszorus *Design Director*

Staff for this Book

John Agnone *Project Editor and Illustrations Editor*

Carolinda E. Averitt *Text Editor*

Lyle Rosbotham *Art Director*

Sallie M. Greenwood *Researcher*

Carl Mehler *Director of Maps*

Jerome N. Cookson *Map Production*

R. Gary Colbert *Production Director*

Richard S. Wain *Production Project Manager*

Cynthia M. Combs, Meredith C. Wilcox *Illustrations Coordinators*

Manufacturing and Quality Control

George V. White *Director*

Alan V. Kerr, Vincent P. Ryan *Managers*

Phillip L. Schlosser *Financial Analyst*

Library of Congress Cataloging-in-Publication Data
Rennicke, Jeff.
   Treasures of Alaska : last great American wilderness / Jeff Rennicke ; photographs by Michael Melford.
      p. cm.
   Includes bibliographical references and index.
   ISBN 0-7922-7876-3 -- ISBN 0-7922-7877-1 (deluxe)
      1. Alaska--Description and travel. 2. Alaska--Pictorial works. 3. Natural history--Alaska. 4. Wilderness areas--Alaska. I. Melford, Michael. II. Title.

F910.5 .R46 2001
917.98--dc21   00-069248

The world's largest nonprofit scientific and educational organization, the National Geographic Society was founded in 1888 "for the increase and diffusion of geographic knowledge." Since then it has supported scientific exploration and spread information to its more than eight million members worldwide.

The National Geographic Society educates and inspires millions every day through magazines, books, television programs, videos, maps and atlases, research grants, the National Geographic Bee, teacher workshops, and innovative classroom materials.

The Society is supported through membership dues, charitable gifts, and income from the sale of its educational products.

Members receive NATIONAL GEOGRAPHIC magazine—the Society's official journal—discounts on Society products, and other benefits.

For more information about the National Geographic Society, its educational programs, publications, or ways to support its work, please call 1-800-NGS-LINE (647-5463), or write to the following address:

National Geographic Society
1145 17th Street, N.W.
Washington, D.C. 20036-4688
U.S.A.

Visit the Society's Web site at
www.nationalgeographic.com

Composition for this book by the National Geographic Society Book Division. Printed and bound by R.R. Donnelley & Sons, Willard, Ohio. Color separations by Quad Graphics, Martinsburg, West Virginia. Dust jacket printed by Miken Companies, Inc., Cheektowaga, New York.